EDISON ETC.

WRITTEN AND ILLUSTRATED BY B.K. HIXSON

DEDICATION

ED GOFFARD

      This is for my fifth grade science teacher at Shaver Elementary School in Parkrose, Oregon. I'm not sure what else we learned that year but we made electric motors, a giant radio, and crystals out of sugar, alum, and copper sulfate. Volcanos blew up and dodecahedrons dominated the skies overhead. My first real taste of science. I will never forget the smell of my electric motor going so fast that it burned up because we ran too much juice through it. Mr Goffard thought it was a good learning experience. I would have, too, if it hadn't taken me the better part of two weeks to build it. In fact, we received the ultimate compliment on our crystal growing ability: someone stole our prize creation . And I am sure I mastered the art of phototropic movement in plants that year. Never could confuse the plant, though.

      I never got the chance to say thank you then, so I am now. You were the best science teacher I ever had because you turned us loose to find the universe on our own. We didn't know we had it so good. Wherever you are I hope that you have some kids to play with. Thanks.

TABLE OF CONTENTS

List of Materials

All the materials that you need to put together a kit to teach any of the activities to the kids.

Acetate sheet, (for overhead projectors)
Alligator clips, 4 of 'em, 12" inches long
Aluminum foil, 1 roll
Baggie, plastic sandwich kind
Balloon, 9 inch round
Balloon, oblong
Battery, D size
Battery, 6 volt
Battery Clip, D size
Beaker, 1000 ml or large glass jar
Bubble kit, 1 bottle with blower, 79¢
Bulb and socket, 1 amp, should have 3
Candle, 6 inches tall , used as handle
Candle, votive, 1
Cardboard, thin, 1 sheet
Clay, 1 lump
Crayons, 1 box
Coat hanger, wire, 3 of 'em
Comb, plastic
Compass
Copper strip, 1/2" by 4" or so
Copper wire, 20-22 gauge, 1 pound
Cork, 1 large enough to fit in jar, see pg. 13
Cork, 1 " in diameter
Dark room, 1
Fluorescent bulb, dead or alive
Foil, metal, thin, eat a candy bar to get it
Glass, drinking, 6 to 12 oz.
Glue, the superglue variety is best
Hammer
Handle, glass or plastic, 12 inches or so
Hydrochloric acid, dilute, 1 pint
Insulating stand
Iron Filings, 4 oz.
Key, metal
Kid, 1, with shoulder length, fine hair
Knife
Lemon, 1 large, fresh
Lid, unpainted, 3 inches in diameter
Light Bulb, 50 -150 watt, 1
Magnet, bar, 2
Magnets, ceramic, 2
Masking tape, 1 roll

Matches, 1 book
Nails, 16 penny, 5
Nails, finishing or paneling, 1 box
Needle, sewing
Newspaper, 1 sheet
Nylon thread, 1 spool
Ruler, either meter or 30 cm
Rod, glass, 12"
Packing peanuts, styrofoam
Paper, steal a sheet from the copy machine
Paperclips, large, 1 box
Paperclips, small, 1 box
Phenolthalein powder
Phonograph record, old, useless
Pie tin
Ping pong ball
Potato, 1 fresh
Puffed rice, 1 box
Rabbit fur, 1
Salt, 1 lb
Scissors
Shoebox lid
Silk, 1 square foot will do
Steel wool, 1 pad, no soap
String, cotton, 1 roll
Test tubes, 2
Tinsel, Christmas tree type, 1 pkg.
Tissue paper, 10 inches long at least
Tweezers, 1 pair
Van de Graff Generator, 1
Vinegar, 1 quart
Washing soda (not baking soda)
Water
Wire cutters, 1 pair
Wool square, 1 square foot will do
Wood blocks, 5 pieces:
      3" x 5" x 1/2"
      3" x 10" x 1/2" (2)
      2" x 3" x 1/2"
      3" x 3" x 1/2"
Zinc strip, 1/2" x 4" or paperclip

THE SCIENTIFIC METHOD

1. Think of an Idea
The first thing that you will need to do is think of an idea for what you will try to explain or do in your experiment, or just something you may want to study. The best way to get started is to adapt an existing experiment in your own unique way.

2. Research Your Topic
Find out what is already known about the topic, and see what you can add to the general body of knowledge.

3. Plan Your Experiment
This section is also called the procedure. You make a game plan of when, where, how, what, and why you are going to do what it is that you are going to do.

4. Experiment
Party time. This is where you get right down to the nitty gritty of doing the experiment, collecting the data, rolling up the sleeves and diving right into the fray.

5. Collect and Record Data
This is all the information that you are seeking, including charts, data tables, illustrations, and records of observations.

6. Come to a Conclusion
Compile the data that you have collected, evaluate the results, come to a conclusion, write a law describing what you observed, and collect your Nobel Prize.

3   Edison Etc.

LAB SAFETY

In every lab class there is always the danger that you may expose yourself to injury. The chemicals and equipment that you use and the way that you use them are very important, not only for your safety but for the safety of those working around you. Please observe the following rules at all times. Failure to do so increases your risk of accident.

1. Goggles.
Goggles should always be worn when chemicals are being heated or mixed. This will protect your eyes from chemicals that spatter or explode. Running water should be available. If you happen to get some chemical in your eye, flush thoroughly with water for 15 minutes. If irritation develops, contact a physician. Take this information with you.

2. Smelling Chemicals.
If you need to smell a chemical to identify it, hold it 6 inches away from your nose and wave your hand over the opening of the container toward your nose. This will "waft" some of the fumes toward your nose without exposing you to a large dose of anything noxious.

3. Chemical Contact With Skin.
Your kit contains protective gloves to wear whenever you are handling chemicals. If you do happen to spill a chemical on your skin, flush the area with water for 15 minutes. If irritation develops, contact a physician. Take the instructions for this kit with you.

4. Clean up all Messes Immediately.
This is no time to be a pig. Your lab area should be spotless when you start experimenting and spotless when you leave. If not, clean it.

5. Proper Disposal of Poisons.
If a poisonous substance is used or formed during the experiments in this lab, the book will tell you. These must be handled according to the directions in the lab guide.

LAB SAFETY

6. No Eating During the Lab.
When you eat, you run the risk of internalizing poison. This is never done unless the lab calls for it. Make sure your hands and lab area are clean.

7. Horse play out.
Horseplay can lead to chemical spills, accidental fires, broken containers, and damaged equipment. Never throw anything to another person; be careful where you put your hands and arms; and no wrestling, punching, or shoving in the lab. Save that for when you get older and start dating.

8. Fire.
If there is a fire in the room notify the person in charge immediately. If they are not in the room and the fire is manageable, smother the fire with a blanket or use an extinguisher in an emergency and send someone to find an adult. REMEMBER: Stop, Drop, and Roll!

9. Better Safe Than Sorry.
If you have questions, or if you are not sure how to handle a particular chemical, procedure, or part of an experiment, ask for help from your instructor or an adult. If you do not feel comfortable doing something, then don't do it. If there is any concern upon chemical exposure, contact a physician.

A WORD ABOUT TEACHING SCIENCE

One of the greatest fears that elementary teachers have about teaching science is that they must know all the answers. Rancid goat excrement. Your job as the teacher is to give the kids opportunities to question, to experiment freely, to wonder, and, most importantly, to solve the mysteries of the universe with a minimum of help from their teacher. Present the ideas in this book to them. Get them to build, to experiment, to play and then ask them why. You have a responsibility to be confused, make erroneous assumptions, and generally disbelieve anything that they tell you without proof. And maybe not even then.

The master of this technique is my friend, Don Peck, a math education professor at the University of Utah. He has been confused for over 30 years and thousands of Utah kids are much better mathematicians for it. An imaginary conversation between Don and kidus generica (your everyday common, classroom kid) would go something like this:

Don: "That looks pretty funny. How did you get the hair on that kid to stand up?"
Kid: "Rubbed it with this balloon."
Don: "Oh, I see. You have a magic balloon."
Kid: "No, I rubbed his head and collected electrons from it and the hairs stand up."
Don: "Why, can't they see sitting down?"
Kid: "No, they all have the same charge and so they repel each other and stand up."
Don: "Hmmmmmm. I'm confused, what causes the hairs to repel?"
Kid: "The electrons."
Don: "I don't see any electrons."
Kid: "You can't; they are invisible. But you can see the result of them being there."
Don: "Oh, I see. The electrons on the balloon attract the hairs?"
Kid: "Yeah, and when the balloon is gone they all have the same positive charge and stand up because like charges repel each other."
Don: "Now I get it. Tell me about this experiment over here...."

He gives the kids a chance to get inside the experiment. Roll it around, beat it up, and get to know it pretty well before he or she has to introduce it to the rest of the class. Your repertoire of questions and comments may include: I don't get it. Why does it do that? Are you sure? I don't believe you. I think you're making that up. How did you figure that out? I'm confused. You can't do that!

Or, my favorite responses to " Mr. Hixson, why does it do that?" are " Beats me. I wasn't paying attention when the teacher explained it." Or " You got me. Do I look like the World Book Encyclopedia today?" All of those comments should be said with a smile in your voice and the kid will figure out right away that their education is their responsibility. As the quote goes, "Spoon feeding teaches nothing more than the shape of the spoon." You do your students a great disservice by telling them the "right answers." Besides, any scientist worth his salt will tell you that nothing in science is ever sacred, everything gets challenged.

There is a limit to all of this stupidity of course, and that limit is set by each teacher. But the bottom line is that science, especially at this level, should be loads of fun, constant inquiry, exciting, and without right or wrong answers until the kid has had time to skin his intellectual knee once or twice trying to unravel the problem. You don't need to know all the answers because the kids will figure it out and teach you if you give them the opportunity. To sum it all up in one word, go play with the kids. That's what you're getting paid for.

PLAY

STATIC ELECTRICITY

A PRIMER

For elementary science the atom is composed of three main parts; we won't get into quarks, muons and other assorted aunts and uncles of the nuclear family. The three biggies are the proton, neutron and electron. The protons and neutrons make up the center of the atom, also called the nucleus, and the electron's job is to bip around on the outside of the atom. Each of these three parts has a different charge. The proton has a positive charge, the neutron is neutral and the electron is negative. When there are the same number of electrons and protons the atom is in a state of electrical balance, or neutral. If there are extra electrons it possesses a negative charge, and if someone has swiped an electron or two, the atom is then said to be positively charged. The drawings on this page should help.

Neutral atom
same number of electrons
and protons

Most of the the experiments that you will be seeing in this section rely heavily on the understanding that like charges repel and opposite charges attract. If you have lots of negatively charged electrons on a balloon, those electrons are going to repel other negative particles and attract positive ones. This causes movement in some cases, and in others you will see odd occurrences in which things stick to walls, float upward when they should fall, and roll across a table as if they were being pulled by some magical force. In every instance it is due to the attraction or repulsion of these small particles. The kids need to remember that this is all influenced by electrons, which are very small, easy to move from one place to another, and cannot be seen.

Positive atom
lost an electron

Two particles that are repulsed by each other

Negative atom
extra electrons

Edison Etc.

HAIRDO GREMLINS

Activity

A rubber balloon will be rubbed on the head of a volunteer from the class. As the electrons accumulate on the surface of the balloon, the volunteer's hair will begin to wig out. You can also stick the balloon to the ceiling, walls, passing secretaries or wool sweaters.

Materials

1   rubber balloon
1   unsuspecting kid

Construction and Use

1. Inflate the balloon. If this is hard for you to do please see your doctor and get checked for tuberculosis, or remember to inhale first. Tie the balloon off. If I don't give that direction invariably some teacher will write and say, "You didn't say to tie the balloon off." If you have trouble ....

2. Select a volunteer from the class. For best results choose a kid that has shoulder length hair that is free of mousse, hair spray or gel. Fine hair tends to work better than coarse hair. This experiment works best on a dry day. The lower the humidity, the better. And remember, blondes may have more fun but the hair color ruins this experiment.

3. Rub the balloon all over the kid's head. As you rub, occasionally lift the balloon up off their head about six inches. Their hair will follow. After about 30 seconds of rubbing, the hair should be sticking up all around. In addition to that, be prepared for a classroom full of howling kids.

4. You can now walk to the wall and stick the balloon to it or, if you want to stand on a chair, put it on the ceiling. If there is someone in the room with a wool sweater on you can hold the balloon to their chest and it will stay there when you release your hand.

What's Goin' On?

Opposite charges (negative and positive) attract and like charges (negative and negative or positive and positive) repel. The balloon has a huge negative charge because it has stolen all these loose electrons and the hair has a huge positive charge because many of its electrons have been stolen. Balloon negative, hair positive, they attract. When you take the balloon out of the picture the hair still tends to stand up on end. This is because each of the hair strands has a positive charge. Like charges repel, and since they can't stand each other, they get as far away from one another as possible. In this case, they stand on end.

Electrons, by nature, are very small and easily lost or stolen from atom to atom. Rubber is a wonderful electron thief. As the rubber balloon is rubbed over the hair of your volunteer, it steals electrons from it. What happens then is that a large excess of electrons builds up on the surface of the balloon and a large debt is being created in the hair. None of the atoms are now balanced.

HAIRDO GREMLINS

When you place the balloon on the wall, ceiling or sweater, the electrons on the balloon cause the electrons in the object to repel. As the electrons repel, the positive charge is exposed. We have a negative balloon and a positive wall; we have attraction. The balloon appears to stick to the wall, but in reality it is the attraction of opposite charges that is responsible for this phenomenon. See the illustration in the Ghost Poop experiment.

Questions to Ask, Things to Try

1. Can we see electrons or are they very small? Show them the balloon after you have rubbed it on the head of the victim.
2. Why do you think the hair is attracted to the balloon?
3. Why does the hair continue to stand on end after the balloon is taken away?
4. Why does the balloon stick to the ceiling, wall or sweater?
5. Invent a machine that uses static electricity.
6. How do you get rid of extra electrons? Is there more than one way?
7. How many different kinds of things can a balloon stick to?
8. How many different kinds of materials will donate electrons to the balloon so that it will stick to the wall?
9. Do blondes have more or fewer electrons than redheads and brunettes? And if they do, who cares?
10. Does the shape of the balloon affect its ability to collect electrons? How could you measure this?

JUMPING PAPER

Activity

A rubber balloon is inflated and electrons are collected from the head of a volunteer. The charged balloon is brought near a pile of small pieces of paper which jump onto the balloon, and then some of those pieces of paper will fly off the balloon into the air.

Materials

1 rubber balloon
1 kid with hair
1 sheet of copy paper
1 pair of scissors

Construction and Use

1. Cut the paper into quarter-inch squares. If you are a little off, that's fine; don't waste your time being precise because it will have little to no bearing on the outcome of the experiment (unless of course you cut squares the size of silver dollars, and then actually those would be circles). Cut small squares.

2. Blow up the rubber balloon, tie it off and swipe some electrons from the head of a kid. If you are doing the activities in order you should be pretty good at this by now. Charge the balloon.

3. Lower the charged balloon toward the pile of paper squares and have fun. The squares will jump onto the balloon and then some of them will jump off again. If you really want to demonstrate the polarity that is established, do this same experiment with pencil shavings. The shavings stand on end when they attach to the balloon and then spring off dramatically after a couple of seconds. One caution: it does get a bit messy with all the pencil lead.

What's Goin' On?

The balloon has a huge negative charge. Said charge is lowered to the paper, which has a balance of negative and positive charges. When the electrons in the paper see the balloon coming, it scares the pee waddlins (something my mom lost a lot of when she was a kid) out of them and they run to the table side of the paper square. This exposes the positive charge, which doesn't care because it is attracted to the negative charge. See the drawing on this page.

JUMPING PAPER

Once the pieces of paper jump onto the balloon they begin to steal electrons from it. This overloads the charge on the paper, making it negative overall. Negatively charged paper on a negatively charged balloon? Not gonna happen for long. The paper jumps off, repelled by the balloon. The paper can't make up its mind. This is like a lot of girls I dated. If you use pencil shavings, the polarity that is established as the shavings "stand up" on the balloon is hilarious. The shavings literally spring off the balloon. Great for a really slow Friday night. Really slow.

Questions to Ask

1. Why did the paper jump up onto the balloon?
2. Does this experiment work if the balloon is not charged first?
3. Why does some of the paper jump off the balloon after it has been there for a while?
4. What other materials will be attracted to the balloon? Write a law of attraction for balloons.
5. Which materials, other than hair, will create a charge on a rubber balloon?
6. Will other objects carry a charge that will attract the pieces of paper?
7. Write a creative essay explaining the perspective of the piece of paper. How does it feel, what does it think, what is its name, how does it get off the balloon, and where does it go and why?

WATER WIGGLER

Activity

A charged balloon is moved back and forth near a stream of running water. The water follows the movement of the balloon.

Materials

1   rubber balloon
1   kid with hair or a piece of wool
1   faucet of running water

water molecule

Construction and Use

1.   Blow up and tie off a rubber balloon. I recommend a 9 to 12 inch balloon for this activity. Charge it on the head of a kid or with a piece of wool. The head is always more desirable.
2.   Turn the water on and bring the balloon close to the stream of water. Observe what happens. Ooooooh aaaaaaaah.

What's Goin' On?

Water, by virtue of the way that it is constructed, is a polar molecule. This means that it acts like a magnet. A small magnet, mini magnet. It has a positive end, and a negative end as illuminated by the diagram on the page. What this means is that as the water molecules fall from the faucet they are free to rotate any way they want. However, since you have a whole stream of magnets flowing out the faucet, all subject to the laws of nature, they are in a fairly orderly pattern. Positive to negative to positive to negative and so on.

When a huge negative charge is brought near this stream of mini magnets, it is going to break up the party. That is why you see the stream bending the way that it does. The charge on the balloon influences the movement of the water molecules.

Questions to Ask, Thing to Try

1.   What do you think causes the water to move?
2.   Find other objects in the room that produce the same effect.
3.   Can you reproduce the same effect using other liquids? What happens if you use vinegar poured out of a can, for example?
4.   What happens if you bring a charged balloon close to a pan full of water? Does the water have to be moving to produce the desired effect?
5.   What objects in the room produce the opposite effect? What did you have to rub them with to get this response?

OBEDIENT PING PONG BALL

Activity

A pocket comb is charged using a piece of wool and then brought close to a ping pong ball. As the comb comes close the ball is attracted to the comb.

Materials

1   ping pong ball
1   plastic comb
1   piece of wool or a sweater will do fine

Construction and Use

1. Rub the comb like crazy with the wool and put a nice healthy charge on it.
2. Set the ping pong ball on a flat table so that it is free to roll around; slowly bring the comb close to it and observe what happens.

What's Goin' On?

The comb has a large negative charge on it when you rub it with the wool. As you bring it close to the ping pong ball which has no charge, the electrons in the comb repel the electrons in the ball, exposing the positive protons. The protons are then attracted to the electrons in the comb and the ball follows the comb. Cool.

Questions to Ask

1. Why do you think the ping pong ball moved?
2. What would happen if you brought a charged rubber balloon close to the ball instead of the comb?
3. What would happen if you used a glass rod charged with a silk cloth close to the ball?
4. Are there other materials that are attracted or repelled the same way by the comb?
5. Write a short story about a machine in a ping pong ball factory that uses this idea. Tell what the machine looks like, how it works and what it does.
6. Substitute a styrofoam ball for the ping pong ball. Do you get the same results? What else can you substitute?

Electric Palm Tree

Activity

A piece of tissue paper that has been cut into long strips is attached to a wire hanger and charged with a balloon or electrophorous. When the charge is commuted down the hanger, the tissue paper strips repel each other, giving the appearance of a palm tree. Way cool, ooooh aaaah.

Materials

1 electrophorous or charged balloon
1 wire coat hanger or thick piece of wire
1 insulating handle, glass or plastic, 12" or so
  glue or a small clump of clay
1 piece of tissue paper that can be cut into quarter-inch thick strips. Should be at least 10 inches long.

Construction and Use

1. Cut the tissue paper into quarter-inch thick strips. If you have eight to ten strips I would say that you have enough.

2. Tape the strips to the end of a wire coat hanger that has been mangled into a straight line. If you have 10-12 gauge copper wire this works well, also.

3. Attach the plastic or glass handle with the glue or clay. Center it on the wire and, if you are using plastic, file a groove into the top of the handle to make it a little sturdier.

4. If you have not made an electrophorous yet turn to that activity on page 19 and put one together. When you do get one, charge it up and touch it to the end opposite the tissue strips.

What's Goin' On?

When the end of the rod is touched with the electrophorous it dumps a bunch of electrons onto the wire. The electrons race to spread out and in so doing many of them wind up on the pieces of tissue paper.

We know that like charges repel so when all of these pieces of tissue paper accumulate a negative charge, they can't stand each other and repel. It looks like the tree comes to life when really it's just a bunch of electrical charges that can't stand each other.

ELECTRIC PALM TREE

Questions to Ask

1. Why did the fronds of the palm tree stick out?
2. Why did the handle have to be made of glass? What if it were made out of metal?
3. Would the tree work just as well if the fronds were shorter? What if they were longer? Ok, skinnier? And now fatter. How about skinnier and longer? You should get the picture by now.
4. List five other materials that you can use to make a tree, other than tissue paper.
5. Write a poem about your palm tree. What kind of coconuts does your tree produce and what just exactly do you find in one of these nuts?
6. How else could you charge the tree?
7. List three ways to remove the charge from the tree.
8. Does the temperature affect the ability of the tree to accumulate or hold a charge? What if you put the tree in an oven? Maybe the cooks will let you experiment in the walk-in cooler at school. How do you measure the effectivness of holding an electric charge? What is your unit of measure? You may have to make one up before you begin.
9. What else can you use for the handle?

ADVERTISING WITH GHOST POOP

Activity

Styrofoam packing material, called peanuts, has been renamed by a group of third grade boys who wish to remain anonymous. We now call it ghost poop. My apologies if you find the name offensive; I think it is quite clever. Anyway, ghost poop is rubbed with either wool or hair so that it accumulates a charge. Once it has a charge it can be stuck on the wall. Repeated application of this process in a predictable pattern yields words. You can go into the principal's office and leave a message on the wall that science is great. It is best to do this only if you have tenure or your husband has been transferred out of state.

Materials

1   quantity (depends on your preference) of ghost poop (styrofoam packing peanuts)
1   source of electrons such as hair or wool
1   principal's office (optional)

Construction and Use

1.   Rub the peanuts with the wool or on the head of the volunteer. A static charge should build up quickly.
2.   Apply the peanuts to a wall, spelling the message that you would like to leave for the next person in the room. On a dry day the peanuts will stay attracted to the wall for several hours.

What's Goin' On?

As the styrofoam is charged, its electrons force the electrons in the wall toward the inside of the wall. Like charges repel. With the positive charges exposed, the magnetic attraction between the wall and the foam allows the foam to stay suspended. Pretty cool, huh? The diagram should take care of any questions. This is just like sticking the balloon to the wall. Exact same concept.

Questions to Ask

1.   What is holding the poop to the wall?
2.   How many different surfaces can hold ghost poop?
3.   Name three different ways to charge the styrofoam. Now name three ways not to charge it.
4.   What happens to the charge when you hold the poop under a stream of running water for ten seconds?
5.   Does humidity affect the ability of the styrofoam to adhere to the wall? Does this experiment work better on a rainy day than a sunny one, or is there any difference?
6.   How long can a styrofoam piece stay on the wall? Do they stay up longer if they are touching one another or if they are separate?
7.   List ten other things that you can charge and stick to the wall. Clean up your mess afterward.

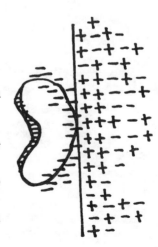

DANCING SOAP BUBBLES

Activity

A plastic comb is given an electric charge by rubbing it with a piece of wool. Soap bubbles are blown into the air and the charged comb is brought near the bubble. With a little practice you can keep the bubble suspended by attracting it upwards with the comb. You are truly a person of mystery when you master this technique.

Materials

1   soap bubble blowing kit
1   plastic comb
1   piece of wool
1   dab of theatrics

Construction and Use

1.   Rub the comb like crazy with the wool and put a really good charge on that puppy (generic term used for informal science materials).
2.   Summon a memory of your kindergarten days and blow a couple of nice soap bubbles. If this was too long ago, enlist the support of one of your students. Bubbles the size of a silver dollar seem to be the best size to learn with. Mastery of the larger bubbles will come with practice, but don't let the neighbors see you.
3.   Once the bubble is in the air bring the comb close to the bubble. The bubble will move in that direction. If you remove the comb before the bubble hits it and bursts, you can keep it suspended for a good long while. It may take a little practice.
4.   After you have played with that for a while, blow a bubble and leave it attached to the plastic bubble blower thing-a-ma-bob. Bring the charged comb close to the bubble and you will notice that the shape of the bubble becomes distorted. If the charge on the comb is strong enough, it may even pull the bubble out of the plastic holder.

What's Goin' On?

The electric charge on the comb attracts the bubble solution, which has both positive and negative particles. The positive particles rotate up and are drawn toward the comb.

Questions to Ask

1.   Why is the bubble attracted to the comb?
2.   What materials, other than wool, can charge the comb so that it will attract the bubble?
3.   Find four other objects that can carry a charge and influence the movement of a soap bubble.
4.   Is the soap bubble attracted to the comb through a piece of paper? How about Saran Wrap?
5.   What kinds of materials insulate against static electricity?

Newspaper Electroscope

Activity

A sheet of newspaper is cut into a thin , one inch wide strip and hung over a ruler. The newspaper is charged with a piece of polyethylene and the two strips repel each other.

Materials

1   sheet of newspaper
1   plastic baggie
1   pair of scissors
1   ruler (either a 30cm or meter stick, I prefer the meter stick)

Construction and Use

1.   Make sure the newspaper is folded and cut a one -inch strip from the edge of it. You should have one very long strip folded in half.

2.   Hang the strip over the ruler and then gently wrap the baggie around the strip near the fold. Pull down briskly. If the two pieces of paper don't repel each other the first time they might by rookies. Give it another couple of tries. As always, the dryer the day the better.

What's Goin' On?

We're back to the same old story again. Like repels like. When you charge the newspaper both halves of it have the same charge. This, as we have seen several times before, does not go over well in nature and they repel each other. For more enlightenment on the topic check the drawing on the page.

Questions to Ask, Things to Try

1.   Why did the two pieces of paper repel each other?

2.   Are there other materials that produce the same effect? If you get stuck on this one try fur, silk and wool for starters.

3.   Can you substitute different kinds of paper for the newspaper and get the same result?

4.   Cut the paper in half and charge each one independently and bring them close together. The same result?

5.   Will this experiment work on a larger scale? Does it work better on a smaller scale? What if you weren't standing on a scale? Do fish scales work? And if so, have we opened up a whole new way of fishing? On a scale of one to ten, how silly is this getting? Next experiment, please.

GLASS JAR ELECTROSCOPE

Activity

The kids will take a small glass jar and construct an electroscope using tin foil, wire and a rubber balloon or electrophorous.

Materials

1   small glass bottle
1   large paperclip
1   sheet of aluminum foil, about one-half square foot will do
1   chewing gum wrapper or other source of thin metal
1   rubber or cork stopper that will fit into the top of the bottle, or tape and a lid.

Construction and Use

1.   If you have a cork, insert the paperclip into the cork. If you don't have a cork, then punch a hole in the lid and insert the paperclip into the lid and secure it with some tape.

2.   Bend the bottom of the paperclip so that it looks like an L. Use the picture as a guide.

3.   Take a piece of aluminum foil from the chewing gum wrapper. Cut it so that it looks like the drawing on page 18 and hang it over the bottom of the L. Insert the whole mess into the jar and secure it with a twist or a good push.

4.   Crumple up the rest of the aluminum and make a ball that will fit on the top of the wire coming out of the jar.

5.   Charge a balloon or a comb and touch it to the aluminum ball at the top of the electroscope. You will see the leaves suddenly separate.

What's Goin' On?

When the electrophorous, or balloon, discharges onto the foil ball at the top of the electroscope jar, the charge disperses over the entire length of the foil and paperclip. This means that we how have two pieces of foil that have the same charge. Like charges repel. Zip... the leaves of foil spread apart. It doesn't get any plainer than that. See the drawing if there is any confusion.

Questions to Ask, Things to Do

1.   Why do the leaves spread apart?
2.   Where does the charge come from that produces this effect?
3.   List three ways to discharge the foil leaves.
4.   Now that you've done that, list three different ways that you can charge the leaves.

DANCING RICE

Activity

Rice puffs suspended on a nylon or silk thread will attract or repel each other when a charged object is brought near them. The kids will be able to make the rice dance and move using static charge.

Materials

1 wire coat hanger
2 grains of puffed rice or two little balls made of cotton
1 piece of tin foil big enough to cover the puffed rice (It is best if this is the kind of tin foil that you get off candy or gum wrappers.)
2 feet of thin silk or nylon thread
1 rubber balloon
1 piece of wool or nylon
1 glass rod
1 piece of silk

Construction and Use

1. Take the piece of thread and tie the rice puffs to each end of it. Once the rice puffs are attached, cover them with the pieces of tin foil.

2. Bend the wire coat hanger into the shape that is shown in the picture on this page, and loop the thread over the rounded part. Shorten the thread so that the rice puffs are a couple of inches off the ground and can swing freely.

3. Bring a charged comb close to the rice puff and touch it so that the charge rubs off onto the puff. Then retract the comb and try to bring it close to the puff again. No matter how hard you try, the puff will always be repelled by the comb until you remove the charge from the rice puff by touching it.

4. Try the same thing with other objects: a balloon, glass rod; use your imagination. If both rice puffs are hanging at the same time they will both aquire the charge and repel each other.

DANCING RICE

What's Goin' On?

This is much like the experiment just before this one. In fact, it is exactly like it with one notable exception. You can eat this one when you're done.

Ladies and gentlemen, we have two unsuspecting grains of puffed rice. Dangling. Poor rice. But they are happy rice because they have a balanced charge. The same number of negatives and positives, electrons and protons if you will. However, when a negative charge is induced on both grains they repel each other. Sad but true, once friends and now can't stand each other.

Resigned to this fate until, miraculously, due to the intervention of a being greater than themselves, the scientist, they are discharged both literally and figuratively. How would you like to have to diagram that last sentence? Round of applause for our assistants, please.

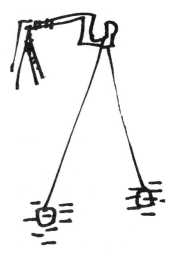

Questions to Ask

1. Why did the rice puffs repel each other?
2. Where does the charge come from that produces this effect?
3. List three ways to discharge the rice puffs.
4. Now that you've done that, list three different ways that you can charge the puffs.
5. What can you substitute for the rice puffs?
6. Do the rice puffs need the foil covering to be effective?
7. Is it possible to charge one rice puff positive and the other negative so that they attract one another? How do you do it?

LOOK MA, NO ELECTRICITY

Activity

A flourescent bulb is rubbed with a piece of wool in a dark room or closet. As the electrons are removed from the surface of the glass, the bulb illuminates. No electricity needed.

Materials

1   flourescent bulb (live or dead, doesn't matter)
1   piece of plastic wrap, polyethylene bag, wool or fur

Construction and Use

Go into a dark closet and shut the door. Hold the flourescent bulb in one hand and the fur or plastic in the other. Rub the bulb vigorously and then pull it away. As the electrons jump the bulb lights up. Who says you can't have good clean fun in a dark closet by yourself?

What's Goin' On?

This activity is a lead in for one of the Van de Graff generator experiments at the end of the book. The information and concepts are the same. The inside of the glass bulb is coated with a white material called phosphor. Phosphor gives off light whenever it is struck by ultraviolet rays. The inside of the bulb is filled with a gas called mercury vapor, which gives off ultraviolet rays when it is excited with electricity. That pretty much sets the stage for the explanation.

When the bulb is rubbed, the plastic wrap steals electrons from the glass and gives it a positive charge. The bulb is then unbalanced and is looking to steal electrons from the nearest available source. This is the gas inside the tube. As the electrons whip through the tube on their way to balance the glass, they collide with the mercury vapor, which releases ultra violet rays, which excites the phosphor, which produces light. Ooooooh aaaaaaah.

It goes back to the one basic idea mentioned in the beginning of the lesson that all things in nature do their dangedest to stay in balance. If we steal electrons from one place it will be looking for a way to get them back. It is this movement that we put to work, in this case to produce light.

Questions to Ask

1.   How was the electricity generated?
2.   Why did the bulb light?
3.   Does a regular incandescent bulb work the same way? Why do you think there is a difference if there is one?
4.   What other materials induce light in the bulb?
5.   Would this experiment work in a vacuum? Yes.

ELECTROPHOROUS

Activity

An electrophorous is an object that will hold a substantial positive charge. It is made using a metal disk and an insulating handle like a glass rod or candle.

Materials

1   candle or glass rod
1   old phonographic record
1   piece of flannel or wool
1   flat unpainted metal disk, about three to five inches in diameter (the top of a soup can or metal jar would work great)

Construction and Use

1. Light a candle and drip candle wax into the center of the inside of the lid. Blow the candle out and stick the base of the candle in the melted wax and hold it there until it hardens. This is your insulated handle.

2. Lay hold of an old beater record. I would suggest possible titles, but don't want to risk alienating all you Box Car Willie fans. Rub the surface of the record with a piece of wool or flannel. You don't have to rub the whole area, just a spot about the same size as the lid that you are going to use. You have now charged your record with a nice negative charge.

3. Set the lid in the area that you have been rubbing and, with a finger from your free hand, touch the top of the lid. This grounds the lid and induces a positive charge.

4. Bring the electrophorous close to a knuckle of the hand that just grounded the lid and, as they say in the Toyota commercials, " Oh, what a feeling!" You will notice a large spark jump from the electrophorous to the joint of your choice.

5. You can recharge the electrophorous several times by simply placing it on the record in the spot that you rubbed and touching the inside of the lid. After a while the record starts to lose its charge and you can recharge it by simply rubbing it again.

ELECTROPHOROUS

What's Goin' On?

The record is rubbed with said flannel, which induces a large negative charge. When the metal disk is brought close to the record, the electrons zip to the other side (also called the top of the lid). What you have done in scientific terms is induce a positive charge on the lid. As the finger of the free hand slowly lowers onto the lid the electrons crowded on the top of the lid jump on and ride up to the wrist. You have grounded the lid, leaving it with a substantial positive charge. When you bring the electrophorous close to the lid, a spark jumps to the closest object and the kids are once again thrilled with your ability to ooooh aaaaah.

Questions to Ask
1. What do you think happens when you touch your finger to the electrophorous?
2. Why is the charge so much stronger than a rubber balloon or a plastic comb?
3. How many times can you recharge the electrophorous before the record gets tired?
4. What happens if you charge the record using a piece of plastic instead of flannel or wool?
5. Does country western charge better than heavy metal?

LEYDEN JAR

Activity

A Leyden jar accumulates and holds a static charge. It works with electricity, a lot like filling a coffee cup with a teaspoon and then spilling the coffee all at once. This jar is made by lining a bottle with aluminum foil, and then filling the jar with static electricity collected with an electrophorous or other item. When the jar is discharged a fairly good spark is given off. Good for getting the attention of any stray cats that happen into the school yard.

Materials

1   plastic tumbler or thin glass, 12 oz. works well
1   piece of aluminum foil large enough to cover the inside of the glass
1   plastic comb
10 paperclips
1   electrophorous (built in the experiment just prior to this one)

Construction and Use

1. Wrap aluminum foil on the outside of the glass so that it goes about three fourths of the way up the side. The tighter, the better.

2. Put aluminum foil on the inside of the glass and wrap it to about the same height as the foil on the outside.

3. Take several paperclips and clip them together. Your chain should be long enough to reach the bottom of the jar with a paperclip or two left over.

4. Lay a comb across the top of the glass and slide the top paperclip into one of the teeth. The chain should drop into the glass and touch the bottom without any problem at all.

5. Take the electrophorous that you made in the experiment just prior to this one and charge it up. Discharge the electrophorous into the Leyden jar by touching the top paperclip. Do this several times to build up the charge.

6. When you are ready to discharge the Leyden jar, touch a short wire to the aluminum foil on the outside of the jar and to the paperclip. You should see a pretty good spark jump across. If you are feeling brave you can discharge the jar by touching one finger to the foil on the outside and another finger on the same hand to the paperclip. Be warned that a pretty good shock could result.

It might be worth noting that Benjamin Franklin killed a large turkey with the electrical shock from a Leyden jar. Also, soon after the advent of the jar, a circle of monks who were experimenting with static electricity held hands while the first monk touched the inside of the jar (which was 6 feet high) and the sixth monk touched the center of the jar. According to the monastic chronicler of the event, "to a man they leaped several feet into the air."

If you are having a hard time getting the jar to work, upgrading the quality of the glass will help. If you use pyrex glass that has been specifically hardened then you may get better results.

©1994 The Wild Goose Company   WG-3009

LEYDEN JAR

What's Goin' On?

Each time the charge is added to the jar it builds up. It is like filling a teacup one spoonful at a time and then spilling the whole cup at once. This instrument is the grandfather of the modern day capacitors which are used extensively in electronics work.

Questions to Ask

1. What do you think is holding the charge in the jar?
2. Why do the paperclips need to go all the way to the bottom of the jar instead of suspending in mid air?
3. What other things can you use to charge the jar (in addition to the electrophorous)?
4. Why can't you make a Leyden jar out of a tin can?
5. Find three other materials that are suitable for holding the charge. If you are stumped, start with an empty milk carton and then try a wooden cigar box, and if you're still lost have the kids brainstorm ideas.
6. Does the jar work if you don't line it with aluminum foil?
7. What happens if you use plastic wrap instead of foil inside the jar? How about wax paper or construction paper? Does newspaper work? Why not?
8. Once the jar is constructed correctly, fill it with water and see if it will accumulate a charge. Add salt if it doesn't work and see what happens.

Magnets

A PRIMER

All of these activities take advantage of the natural interaction between the opposite ends of a magnet. Like poles repel and opposite poles attract. The other element that is introduced is that iron exhibits a response to the magnetic field. Other metals (gold, silver, tin, aluminum, brass, and so on) are not influenced. This attraction is used to demonstrate the extent of the field of a magnet and produce several illusions.

WHAT IS MAGNETIC?

Activity

The kids will take an ordinary bar magnet and rip around the room collecting information about what is attracted to the magnet and what isn't. They will then write a law of magnetism based on the information they have collected.

Materials

1   bar magnet
1   circular magnet (optional)
2   pairs of beady eyes and a pad to record observations on

Construction and Use

1.   Have the kids list the following categories on a sheet of paper and leave ten spaces under each one: metal, wood, glass, plastic, cloth and living. Instruct the kids to test ten objects from each of these categories and circle the objects that were attracted to the magnet. I'd give the little curtainhangers no more than 15 minutes and I'd eyeball 'em at ten.

2.   After they have collected the information, have them sit down and write the data that they have collected on the board. You should have no attraction to the magnet from any of the categories other than metal. But not all of the metal tested should be attracted to the magnet.

3.   Have them test the metal objects again, but as best as possible decide what metal they are testing. In a classroom you should find iron, tin, aluminum, brass, gold or silver on the teacher, and possibly some zinc, but that is usually found as an alloy with iron so it won't stand out as a pure metal.

What's Goin' On?

Only iron, cobalt, nickel, and a few other metals exhibit magnetic properties. The kids will soon discover that glass, wood, plastic, cloth, any natural fiber or tissue, and some metals will not attract. The iron particles have the built in characteristics that allow them to align into positive and negative and respond to the magnet.

Questions to Ask

1.   Which things are attracted to a magnet and which things are not?

2.   Are all metal objects attracted to the magnet?

3.   What kinds of metals are and what kinds are not?

4.   Are things attracted to the magnet if they have to travel through a piece of paper?

5.   Does the shape of the magnet affect the ability of the magnet to pick up items?

LINES OF FORCE

Activity

A modified shoe box lid is placed over a bar magnet and iron filings are sprinkled onto it to reveal the lines of force radiating from the magnet. Oooooh Aaaaaah.

Materials

1   shoe box lid
1   container of iron filings
1   roll of masking tape
1   acetate (overhead) sheet
1   pair of scissors

Construction and Use

1. Cut a square out of the lid so that it looks like the drawing. Tape the acetate sheet into the inside of the lid. If it is too big, cut it down a bit.
2. Place a magnet on the table and put the lid on top of it in the center.
3. Sprinkle iron filings on the acetate. Be generous in your use of the filings; you will be able to recycle them. Once you have the filings in the lid, gently tap the edge of the shoebox and the filings will align in the natural pattern of the lines of force.
4. When you are done, all you have to do is lift the lid up and pour the filings into the container that they came from.

What's Goin' On?

All magnets produce invisible lines of force that radiate from the ends (or poles) of the magnet. These lines of force can be inferred by iron particles, which act like miniature magnets themselves. When the filings are sprinkled on the sheet, they line up with the lines of force and actually show where the lines are strongest.

When you are all done, picking the lid up removes the filings from the presence of the magnetic force, and they can be poured back into their container without any problem at all. Or, as they say in Jamaica, "No problem, mon."

LINES OF FORCE

Questions to Ask

1. Where are the lines of force convergent? Where do they come together?
2. Why did you put the shoebox lid over the magnet? What happens if you don't?
3. Take the magnet and run it around the inside of the box. What happens to the lines of force?
4. Flip the magnet around a couple of times and watch the iron filings very closely. Why do the filings flip with the magnet?
5. Can you see the lines of force if you don't put an acetate sheet in the lid but rather leave it intact? Why do we put the acetate sheet into the lid in the first place?
6. Where is the magnet the strongest? Why do you think this is the strongest place (or places)?
7. Where is the magnet the weakest? How can you tell that the magnet is weak in this place (or places)?
8. Invent a machine that uses the attraction of iron particles to help it do its job.

MAGNETS & COMPASSES

Activity

A compass is moved around a bar magnet to demonstrate the lines of force that radiate from the magnet. The kids will observe that a magnet has two different poles and map the lines of force.

Materials

1   compass
1   bar magnet
1   pencil and paper

Construction and Use

1.   Place a plain piece of white paper on the table in front of you. Put the bar magnet in the middle of the paper and trace around it. Make ten dots around the magnet and number them.

2.   Place the compass on each of the spots and draw an arrow showing which way the north end of the compass is pointing.

3.   Move the compass out one inch from the dots and repeat this procedure. And then move it out 2 inches from the dots and repeat it one more time.

4.   When you are all done connect the dots for each of the three markings and you should have a pretty good idea of what the magnetic lines of force look like. This is a good follow-up activity for the experiment just prior to this one: Lines of Force.

What's Goin' On?

The compass is influenced by the lines of force radiating from the magnet. As the lines of force bend, the compass will turn to reflect this movement.

Questions to Ask

1.   What is causing the compass to move back and forth?

2.   What happens to the north pole of the compass as you move it around the magnet in a circle?

3.   Place a circular magnet in the center of the paper and try to map the lines of force for it. After you have done that, try a horseshoe magnet. Compare the lines of force for all three.

4.   Where do you think the lines of force are the strongest and where do you think that they are the weakest? What evidence do you have that supports these ideas?

5.   How far out does the magnet affect the compass? How can you tell that there is no more effect on the compass?

MAKING A COMPASS

Activity

A needle is magnetized with a bar magnet and floated on a thin cork in water. This is a crude compass.

Materials

1 bar magnet
1 steel needle
1 pie tin
1 cork
  water
1 knife

Construction and Use

1. Take the cork and cut it down so that it is about a quarter of an inch thick and then float it in the pan of water.
2. Take the needle and rub it 50 times in one direction with the magnet. Think of this as the same way that you would comb your hair. You wouldn't go back and forth; the making of a compass is the same way.
3. Once you have magnetized the needle by rubbing it with the magnet, place it on the center of the cork. Bring the magnet near the compass and see if it will respond as you move it back and forth.

What's Goin' On?

The needle acts like a little magnet because it is made of iron. When you rub the needle, the magnet lines up the iron atoms in it so that they are all headed the same direction. It is a lot like the kids when they are playing outside for recess and the teacher blows the whistle and lines are formed so that they can come inside. As the magnet is moved around, the needle follows the same way that a compass would move. If the needle is left alone it will point to magnetic north and can be checked with a standard compass.

Questions to Ask

1. Does the needle respond to the magnet before it has been rubbed?
2. What do you think happens to the needle when it is rubbed by the magnet?
3. How can you tell that the needle has been magnetized?
4. Take a needle that hasn't been magnetized and lay it along the magnet for about 5 minutes. Without rubbing it at all, take it and put it on the cork and see if it has been magnetized.
5. What other materials can be used to create a magnet?

PLAYING WITH POLES

Activity

A bar magnet is suspended from a string. Another bar magnet is brought close to the magnet. The first time it attracts the suspended magnet, the second time it repels it. Only our caped crusaders know why; stay tuned to this bat experiment in this bat book.

Materials

2   bar magnets
1   12" piece of string
1   edge of a table
1   roll of masking tape

Construction and Use

1. Tie the end of the string around the middle of one of the bar magnets. Tape the other end of the string to the table so that the magnet swings freely below it.
2. Hold the other bar magnet in your hand so that the north end (there's an N on that side) is exposed. Twist the suspended magnet so that the south end (you guessed it, the S side) is pointing toward you. Bring the south and north ends close together and see what the reaction is.
3. Now reverse the suspended magnet so that the north side is facing toward you and bring the north side of the magnet toward it. Note the reaction.
4. Repeat steps two and three using the south side of the magnet in your hand.

What's Goin' On?

As you bring the south end of the magnet close to the north end of the suspended magnet, there is an attraction. When you flip the magnet in your hand around and bring the north end close to the north end that is suspended it repels it. Exercise of the basic ideas of magnetism: opposites attract and likes repel.

Questions to Ask

1. What happens when a positive end is brought close to another positive end of a magnet?
2. What happens when a negative end is brought close to another negative end of a magnet?
3. What happens when the positive end of a magnet is brought close to the negative end of a magnet?
4. Invent a machine that pushes objects using magnetic repulsion. Explain how the machine works and what it is used for.
5. Figure out a way to get the bar magnet that is suspended swinging. Once it has started, figure out three ways to get it stopped.

FLYING PAPERCLIP

Activity

A paper clip attached to a string taped to the table is suspended in mid-air by a magnet. Sounds like one of those songs you learn at summer camp doesn't it?

Materials

1   paper clip
1   12-inch piece of string
1   roll of masking tape
1   bar magnet

Construction and Use

1.   Tie the string to the paper clip and tape the end of the string to the table. If the paper clip is taped to the table at this point you need to tape the other end. The paper clip should be swinging freely.
2.   Take the magnet and hold it over the table. Using your other hand, lift the paper clip up toward the magnet. When you get it close enough the paper clip will be attracted to the magnet and appear to be suspended in mid-air.

What's Goin' On?

The iron in the paper clip is attracted to the magnet. I wish it were more complex than that, but we have pretty much covered all the bases with that one sentence.

Questions to Ask

1.   Why is the paper clip suspended in mid-air?
2.   How many other things can you attach to a string and suspend with a magnet?
3.   What happens if you try this experiment without the string?
4.   Is the experiment altered by using a circular magnet? How about a horseshoe magnet?
5.   Can you get the paper clip swinging in a circle without touching it with the magnet or swinging the string with your hand?

INVINCIBLE ATTRACTION

Activity

The kids are going to experiment with a compass and a magnet to demonstrate that the magnetic field permeates most things.

Materials

1   bar magnet
1   compass
1   room full of goodies
1   pile of paper clips
1   square foot of cloth materials

Construction and Use

This is a turn 'em loose activity. Give each team of kids a magnet and let them explore the room for objects to test. Their objective is to find as many things as they can that a magnetic field can permeate and still attract an iron object. To demonstrate the activity hold up a magnet and a piece of cloth. Wrap the magnet in the cloth and dip it into a pile of paper clips. The kids will see that the paper clips are attracted to the magnet through the cloth. Ask the kids to test wood, paper, cloth, glass, metal, gerbil hide, anything that they can think of that won't make a mess.

What's Goin' On?

The magnetic field of a magnet or a wire that has electric current running through it doesn't pay any attention to conventional boundaries. Depending on the strength of the magnet, it will permeate most anything and continue its influence.

Questions to Ask

1. Have the kids list the objects that the magnet could permeate and the ones that it couldn't on the board. Ask them to write a "law " of magnetic attraction based on their findings.

2.. If you put two magnets side by side and hold them near an object that previously would not allow you to attract an iron object through it, will it now work? Why or why not?

3. Put a paper clip in a glass of water and ask the kids to get it out without getting their fingers wet or spilling the water.

4. Have them invent a magnetic tool that will pick up iron without coming in direct contact with the object that needs to be picked up.

5. Have the kids write a story from the perspective of the magnetic field. What does it feel like to go through different things to pick up iron objects? What does it think when it gets stopped or the object that it is going through is too thick to permeate? How about if the object is very light or too heavy?

PAPERCLIP FREEWAY

Activity

The kids are going to make paper cars and attach paper clips to the undersides of them. Then they are going to construct a freeway or town or country road and "drive" the cars using a magnet that they move on the underside of the paper.

Materials

1   sheet of paper, 11" x17"
1   paper clip per car they are going to construct
1   bar magnet
1   pair of scissors
1   box of crayons
1   roll of masking tape

bottom   top

Construction and Use

1. Cut a one-inch strip off the end of the sheet of paper. This will be your car construction material. Have the kids color a car on the strip and cut it out. If they are interested, have them do more than one kind of car; include trucks or mototcycles if they want. Under each car have the kids tape a paper clip.

2. Next step is to have them construct a road system of some sort. It can be a country road, city street, freeway system, anything. Encourage them to put in parks or skyscrapers or rivers; make it an interesting and creative exercise.

3. Place the cars on the roads and play. If you are feeling ambitious you can even do a little early childhood driver training and teach them the proper way to proceed at a four way stop, how to make turns, etc.

What's Goin' On?

The iron in the paperclip is attracted to the magnet. As the magnet moves under the paper, the paperclip follows, giving the illusion that the cars are moving on their own power.

Questions to Ask

1. Why does the car move?
2. Do magnetic lines of force go through different materials or do they just move through air? How do we know this?
3. Find three other materials that you can put on the bottom of the cars to attract them to the magnet.
4. Does it matter what end of the magnet you use to pull the car around the freeway? What happens if you pull the car one way and then flip the car around and pull it with the other end?
5. What other kinds of games can you make using the same idea?

MAGNETIC SEPARATOR

Activity

The kids are going to use a magnet to separate salt from iron filings. This is a way of introducing one of the characteristics used to identify chemical compounds.

Materials

1   bar magnet
1   piece of plastic wrap
1   roll of masking tape
1   baggie with a teaspoon of iron filings and teaspoon of salt mixed together.

Construction and Use

1.   Take the piece of plastic wrap and wrap it around the end of the magnet and tape it in place. This makes clean up a lot easier, because instead of dipping the magnet directly into the iron and then having to deal with a bearded magnet, you can simply remove the plastic wrap and the iron falls off. Pretty snazzy, huh?

2.   Shake the baggie up so that the iron and the salt are thoroughly mixed and either empty the contents onto the table or roll the baggie down so that the contents are exposed.

3.   Lower the magnet (the end covered with the plastic wrap) into the pile of iron and salt and lift it out. You should only have iron on the end of the magnet and the salt will have remained on the table.

What's Goin' On?

It's a matter of simple attraction. The iron filings, made out of iron atoms, are attracted to the magnet and the salt, made out of sodium and chlorine, isn't. The reason that you put the plastic or piece of paper over the magnet is so that it is easier to clean up when you are done.

Questions to Ask

1.   Why did the magnet lift the iron filings off the table, but not the salt?

2.   Invent a machine that uses this principle and tell what it would be used for.

3.   What happens if you mix sugar with iron filings? Does it change the way things work at all?

4.   Find another combination of materials that acts this way.

5.   If you want to get really fancy, heat the sugar and iron in a pyrex test tube over a propane flame or a sterno stove until the sugar melts. Put a cloth over the test tube and break it with a hammer, and remove the lump of iron and sugar. Test it for magnetic properties. You should find that the iron has lost its ability to respond to the magnet.

ELECTRICITY

A PRIMER

Electricity is the name we give to the movement of electrons from one place to another. In the experiments that we will be performing with the kids, this is always chemically induced. A material that has lots of extra electrons donates them to a material that does not. These electrons will be subject to movement through different pathways, series and parallel circuits, different materials, electrolytes, and different objects that make use of their movement to produce light, heat, or a sound. This section introduces the kids to all of those concepts. Go team.

CONDUCTORS & INSULATORS

Activity

A simple circuit is constructed to test objects and determine if they are conductors of electricity or insulators.

Materials

1   battery (preferably in a battery clip)
3   alligator clips or 3 12" lengths of copper wire, 20-22 gauge
1   1 amp bulb with socket
1   room full of goodies to test

Construction and Use

1.   Insert the battery into the battery clip. If you don't have a battery clip I highly recommend one because it will save you the hassel of trying to tape the clips to the battery. You will notice that the clip has two terminals and each terminal has a small rotating aperature with a hole in it. Check the diagram . This is where you attach the alligator clip or insert the end of the copper wire. If you attach the wire to any other part it will not draw a current because the rest of the clip is insulated by the rubber washers that you see on the ends.

2.   Attach one alligator clip to each end of the battery clip. Again I would recommend alligator clips over copper wires because the kids will have an easier time attaching them and the wires tend to pop out of the battery clip. You should now have two alligator clips or two wires attached to the two ends of the battery clip.

3.   Attach one of the ends of those alligator clips, it doesn't matter which in, to one of the terminals on the socket. Take the third alligator clip that was previously unattached and connect it to the other terminal of the light bulb. If you set this out in a straight line you should have three alligator clips with a battery or lamp in between each clip. Use the diagram as a guide, it usually is a lot less confusing than written directions.

4.   Touch the two loose leads together and observe that the light will come on. This means that electricity is flowing through the circuit. Use the leads to test different materials and determine if they are conductors or insulators. You do this by attaching or touching the leads to the material. If the light comes on you've got a conductor and if it doesn't it is an insulator.

5.   Once the conductivity testers are working have the kids find 50 conductors and 50 insulators. It won't take as long as you think.

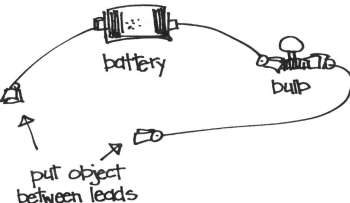

CONDUCTORS & INSULATORS

Trouble Shooting

If the light doesn't light up when you touch the two leads together check the following things in this order:

1. Make sure the light bulb is screwed in all the way. Sometimes the bottom of the bulb is not touching the contact in the base of the socket.

2. Check to make sure that the alligator clips or the wires are attached to the terminals of the battery clip or battery and not to the base or the sides of the battery.

3. Check the bulb in a system that works; sometimes the kids hook three or more batteries in series and blow the bulbs and don't tell you.

4. Check the battery in a system that works; if the battery has been around for a while it is possible that it may be out of juice.

5. Occasionally an alligator clip develops a crack in the wire and becomes separated. If everything else is working and you still don't get a light, check the alligator clips in a system that is working.

6. If the bulb still doesn't light throw everything away and start a unit on weather or geology.

What's Goin' On?

A conductor is a material that allows electricity to flow through it. An insulator is an object that does not allow electricity to flow through it. As the kids experiment they will find that all metal objects are conductors and that all other items tested are insulators. The structure of metal atoms allows them to have the ability to pass electrons from one to another. Often times I hear people explain that the electrons are passed like a water balloon or orange in a relay race. A better model would be to think of the metal as hose that is full of water and when you turn it on water shoots out the end immediately. Metal is full of electrons that are both ready and free to move, so when the juice is turned on we see an immediate reaction.

Questions to Ask

1. What kinds of materials are conductors and which are insulators?
2. Write a "law" that allows you to identify a conductor and tell it from an insulator.
3. Is it possible to turn a conductor into an insulator or an insulator into a conductor? How did you do it?
4. List ten places where insulators would be helpful and ten where they wouldn't be any good at all.
5. List ten places where conductors would be helpful and ten where they wouldn't be of any help at all.
6. Invent a machine that has both conductors and insulators placed on it and tell what the machine does and how much it costs to run the machine for a day.

SERIES CIRCUIT

Activity

Two or three light bulbs are hooked up in series to demonstrate the characteristics of a series circuit.

Materials

    2 or 3 light bulbs with sockets
    3 or 4 alligator clips or 3 or 4 pieces of wire, 20-22 gauge (12" is fine)
    1 battery (preferably in a battery clip)

Construction and Use

1. Insert the battery into the battery clip. If you don't have a battery clip I highly recommend one because it will save you the hassel of trying to tape the clips to the battery. You will notice that the clip has two terminals and each terminal has a small rotating aperature with a hole in it. Check the diagram . This is where you attach the alligator clip or insert the end of the copper wire. If you attach the wire to any other part it will not draw a current because the rest of the clip is insulated by the rubber washers that you see on the ends.

2. Attach one alligator clip to each end of the battery clip. Again I would recommend alligator clips over copper wires because the kids will have an easier time attaching them and the wires tend to pop out of the battery clip. You should now have two alligator clips or two wires attached to the two ends of the battery clip.

3. Attach one of the ends of those alligator clips, it doesn't matter which end, to one of the terminals on the socket. Take the third alligator clip that was previously unattached and connect it to the other terminal of the light bulb. If you set this out in a straight line you should have three alligator clips with a battery or lamp in between each clip.

4. Hook another bulb up to the loose alligator clip ends. You should now have two bulbs, three alligator clips and one battery all forming a giant circle. This is the completed series circuit.

5. Unscrew one of the bulbs, it doesn't matter which, and observe what happens to the whole system. Screw that bulb back in and unscrew the other one and see what happens this time.

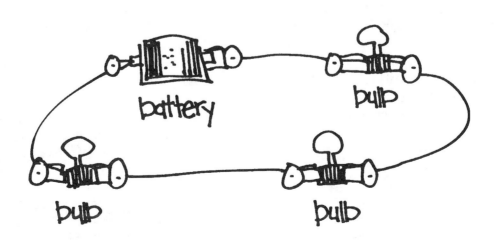

SERIES CIRCUIT

Trouble Shooting

If the light doesn't light up when you touch the two leads together check the following things in this order:

1. Make sure the light bulb is screwed in all the way. Sometimes the bottom of the bulb is not touching the contact in the base of the socket.

2. Check to make sure that the alligator clips or the wires are attached to the terminals of the battery clip or battery and not to the base or the sides of the battery.

3. Check the bulb in a system that works; sometimes the kids hook three or more batteries in series and blow the bulbs and don't tell you.

4. Check the battery in a system that works; if the battery has been around for a while it is possible that it may be out of juice.

5. Occasionally an alligator clip develops a crack in the wire and becomes separated. If everything else is working and you still don't get a light, check the alligator clips in a system that is working.

6. If the bulb still doesn't light throw everything away and start the literature assignment that you're planning on introducing next week.

What's Goin' On?

The electricity is flowing through all of the items in the circuit. This is the way the old Christmas tree lights worked. If one of the lights went out, the whole system was shorted out. There are no alternative pathways like there are in a parallel circuit.

Questions to Ask/Things to Do

1. What happens when you unscrew one of the bulbs in the series? Why do you think this happens?

2. Attach one of the alligator clips to the base of the battery clip instead of the terminal that is made for that purpose. What happens and why do you think that it happens?

3. Add another battery to the circuit and see what happens to the intensity of the light coming from the bulbs.

4. Remove one bulb completely from the circuit and see what happens to the intensity of the light.

5. Predict how much light each of the bulbs would emit if you added a third bulb to the experiment. Do it and see if your prediciton was correct.

6. Try mixing two bulbs and two batteries in different combinations and see if the intensity of the light changes when the bulbs are together or separated by batteries. Should this make any difference? Why or why not?

PARALLEL CIRCUIT

Activity

The kids will construct and demonstrate the characteristics of a parallel circuit using two or three light bulbs.

Materials

2 or 3 light bulbs with sockets
3 or 4 alligator clips or 3 or 4 pieces of wire (20-22 gauge), 12" is fine
1 battery (preferably in a battery clip)

Construction and Use

1.   Insert the battery in the battery clip. If you don't have a battery clip I highly recommend one because it will save you the hassel of trying to tape the clips to the battery. You will notice that the clip has two terminals and each terminal has a small rotating aperture with a hole in it. Check the diagram . This is where you attach the alligator clip or insert the end of the copper wire. If you attach the wire to any other part it will not draw a current because the rest of the clip is insulated by the rubber washers that you see on the ends.

2.   Attach one alligator clip to each end of the battery clip. Again I would recommend alligator clips over copper wires because the kids will have an easier time attaching them and the wires tend to pop out of the battery clip. You should now have two alligator clips attached to the two ends of the battery clip.

3.   Attach one of the ends of those alligator clips, it doesn't matter which end, to one of the terminals on the socket. Take the third alligator clip that was previously unattached and connect it to the other terminal of the light bulb. If you set this out in a straight line you should have three alligator clips with a battery or lamp in between each clip.

4.   Hook the loose alligator clip to the bulb terminal. You should get light at this point. If you don't, zip down to the trouble shooting section of this lab.

5.   Attach two more alligator clips to the alligator clips that are hooked onto the bulb. Insert another lamp where these two clips come together. What your lab should look like is two loops radiating from a battery. A diagram at this point could be very helpful.

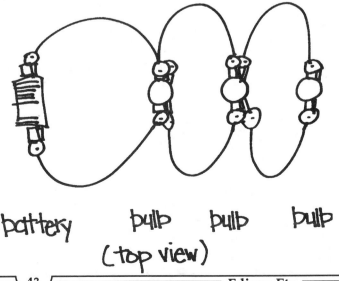

battery   bulb   bulb   bulb
(top view)

PARALLEL CIRCUIT

Trouble Shooting

If the light doesn't light up when you touch the two leads together, check the following things in this order:

1. Make sure the light bulb is screwed in all the way. Sometimes the bottom of the bulb is not touching the contact in the base of the socket.

2. Check to make sure that the alligator clips or the wires are attached to the terminals of the battery clip or battery and not to the base or the sides of the battery.

3. Check the bulb in a system that works; sometimes the kids hook three or more batteries in series and blow the bulbs and don't tell you.

4. Check the battery in a system that works; if the battery has been around for a while it is possible that it may be out of juice.

5. Occasionally an alligator clip develops a crack in the wire and becomes separated. If everything else is working and you still don't get a light, check the alligator clips in a system that is working.

6. If the bulb still doesn't light throw everything away and start a unit on weather or geology.

What's Goin' On?

The electricity is given the opportunity to travel in several different pathways, as opposed to just one like in the series circuit. This means that if the electricity zips along the wires and hits a dead end it can take a detour and still get the job done.

Questions to Ask

1. What happens when you unscrew one of the bulbs in the circuit? Why do you think this happens?

2. Attach one of the alligator clips to the base of the battery clip instead of the terminal that is made for that purpose. What happens and why do you think that it happens?

3. Add another battery to the circuit and see what happens to the intensity of the light coming from the bulbs.

4. Now add that battery in parallel and not series and see what happens to the intensity of the bulbs.

5. Remove one bulb completely from the circuit and see what happens to the intensity of the light.

6. Predict how much light each of the bulbs would emit if you added a third bulb to the experiment. Do it and see if your prediction was correct.

7. Put the bulbs in a parallel series with batteries and see what happens to the intensity of the light.

ELECTROMAGNET

Activity

An ordinary 16 penny nail is transormed into an electromagnet that can pick up anything that has iron in it.

Materials

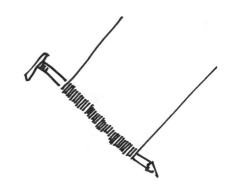

1   16 penny nail
1   6 volt lantern battery
2   alligator clips (optional)
3   feet of copper wire (20-22 gauge),
     should be enameled or insulated
1   pair of wire cutters (optional)
1   pile of paper clips or straight pins

Construction and Use

1.   Make sure that the nail is relatively free from rust. Leave an eight inch tail on the wire and begin wrapping the nail with wire. The magnet works best if the wraps are close to each other and wound tightly next to the nail. If you get to the end of the nail and you have extra wire, cut it off with the wire cutters, leaving another eight inch tail.

2.   Dip the electromagnet in the pile of paper clips and see if it picks any up. It shouldn't.

3.   Attach two alligator clips to the terminals of a 6 volt battery and then attach one lead to each of the tails on your electromagnet. There is a picture lest there be any confusion. The juice should be flowing.

4.   Dip the electromagnet in a pile of pins or paper clips and see what happens now.

What's Goin' On?

When electricity flows through a wire, a magnetic field is induced. As the electricity flows through a nail that has lots and lots of wires wrapped around it, a rather large magnetic effect is produced. When this electrically driven magnet (hence the name electromagnet) is brought close to the pile of pins, they are

ELECTROMAGNET

Questions to Ask

1. Why didn't the electromagnet work when it wasn't hooked up to the battery? What does the electricity do to make the nail into a magnet?

2. How many pins can you pick up with your electromagnet?

3. Rewrap your electromagnet using the same wire that you had, but this time make the wraps loose and sloppy. Hold it next to the pile of pins once you have hooked it back up to the battery and see if you can pick up the same number of pins.

4. Unhook the electromagnet from the battery and see if the magnet can still pick up iron objects.

5. Why is this tool called an electromagnet and not just a plain magnet?

6. Try to make electromagnets out of the following materials: wooden pencil, metal spoon, plastic straw, wooden tree limb, metal fork and rubber eraser. Which things worked and which did not?

7. Write a rule about what materials you can use to make electromagnets and those that you can't. You may want to remind the kids or follow up this activity with the conductors and insulators activity.

FUSES

Activity

The role of a fuse to protect a circuit is demonstrated. A simple series circuit is constructed and then shorted using a pair of tweezers to demonstrate how fuses are blown. A second way of demonstrating fuses is explained using steel wool.

Materials

1   battery with clip (you may want a second battery for extra juice)
2   alligator clips or 12 inch pieces of copper wire
1   bulb and lamp
1   strand of Christmas tree tinsel
1   pad of extra fine steel wool
1   pair of tweezers

Construction and Use

1.   Hook a battery, a bulb, a piece of Christmas tree tinsel, and three alligator clips together so that they match the picture on the page.
2.   When you hook these together the bulb should light. Now take the tweezers and short the system by touching the two terminals of the bulb. The tinsel should melt. You just blew a fuse.
3.   Another way of demonstrating this is to use a strand of steel wool in place of the tinsel. The difference is that the steel wool may short the instant you connect the battery to the alligator clip.
4.   If you're having a tough time getting the fuse to blow, use two batteries in series or a 6 volt.

What's Goin' On?

A fuse is designed to protect sensitive or expensive electrical equipment from surges in the power supply that would destroy them. They also serve to protect wire and equipment from getting too much juice, overheating and catching on fire.

In this experiment you are shorting the circuit by touching the two terminals with the tweezers. The electricity flows through the wire very fast and there is too much for the tinsel to handle so it frizzels. This ideally protects the bulb from getting too much juice.

Questions to Ask

1.   Why didn't the fuse blow when the battery was hooked up?
2.   What happened when the tweezers were touched to the two terminals of the light bulb?
3.   Find two other materials that make good fuses.
4.   List three different kinds of tools or instruments that use fuses to protect them from too much electricity.
5.   Find out where the fuse box or circuit breaker is in your house and find out as much information about that place as you can. Tell what you could do to get the electricity going in your house again if the fuses or circuits blew.

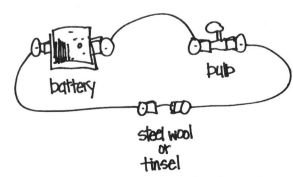

MINI HEATER

Activity

A short copper wire is wrapped between the positive and negative terminals of a battery. As the electrons flow through the wire, the resistence of the wire causes some of the energy to be lost as heat. This heat can be felt by touching the wire.

Materials

1   6 volt lantern battery
1   8 inch piece of bare copper wire (20-22 gauge)

Construction and Use

1. Pass a small piece of copper wire around to the class and have them describe it for you. Pay special attention to the temperature.
2. Hook the wire to a 6 volt battery like the one that is pictured on this page and, after 30 seconds, have the kids touch the wire and describe the temperature.

What's Goin' On?

As electrons flow through the wire they bump into the copper atoms. When they bump they produce a little heat. The retardation of electron movement is called resistence. Different wires have different resistences and are used as tools in electrical instruments to prevent too much electricity from getting to a certain place at a certain time.

What you have made here is a mini heater. Larger heaters work on the same principle of slowing the electrons down with resistence and producing heat in the process. Have the kids be careful when they are touching the wire because it can get very hot.

Questions to Ask

1. Why wasn't the wire hot when it was just sitting on the table not hooked up to the battery?
2. What is going through the wire to make it feel hot?
3. Use other wires of differing thicknesses and see if they heat up more quickly or slowly.
4. Use different kinds of wire (copper, zinc, brass, steel) and see if they heat up at different rates.
5. Write a poem about a wire the gets hooked up to a battery and gets very hot.

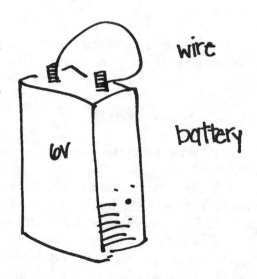

wire

battery

6v

ELECTROCHEMISTRY

A PRIMER

The underlying principle of electrochemistry is that certain ions (charged atoms) in a solution can be electrically directed from one place to another. We are once again taking advantage of the fact that opposites attract. For example, we know that copper ions (charged atoms) have a positive charge. So let's say that we dump a whole bunch of these atoms into a glass and let them float around. They will do just that, float around, until we put two electrodes, positive and negative, in the solution and turn the juice on. Once there is a current in the solution the copper ions are going to be attracted or "directed", if you will, toward the negative electrode. It is a lot like kids at recess. For 15 minutes they are milling, running and jumping all over the place and then the buzzer sounds. Everyone lines up and knows where to go. Well, almost everyone.

ELECTROLYSIS OF WATER

Activity

Water is separated into hydrogen and oxygen gases by running an electric current through it. The individual gases can be collected at the electrodes and ignited to demonstrate their individual characteristics.

Materials

1   large glass jar
1   source of water
2   copper wires, 20-22 gauge
2   test tubes
1   book of matches
1   6 volt battery
     sodium sulfate
     bromothymol blue indicator
     dilute sulfuric acid

Construction and Use

1. Fill the glass jar with water, two thirds full should do the trick. Stir in a couple of teaspoons of sodium sulfate. Add a drop or two of bromothymol blue indicator.

2. Hook the two copper wires to the battery and then put them in the solution, making sure that they don't touch. Bubbles should begin to form on each wire with a yellow color around one wire and a blue color at the other.

3. Invert two test tubes full of water and place one over each copper lead. The purpose of these is to collect gasses that are being produced at each lead.

4. When the test tubes are full of gas you can test its flammability. Light a match and gently lift one of the test tubes up and insert the match. If the match starts to burn brighter, you have just exposed it to oxygen that was collected at the positive terminal. If there was a pop and a blue flame, you lit hydrogen gas collected at the negative terminal. Note the color that formed at each test tube of gas.

5. If you would like to speed the reaction up, add a dash of sulfuric acid to the solution. This acid should be used in diluted form and I would refrain from letting the children even come in contact with it.

ELECTROLYSIS OF WATER

What's Goin' On?

As the electricity passes through the wires, it causes the water molecules to separate into ions and gas molecules. The hydrogen ions, which are positively charged, and oxygen gas form at the positive terminal. The hydroxide ions, which are negatively charged, and hydrogen gas form at the negative terminal. Once the gases reach their respective terminals they collect together in large enough mass to form a bubble and float up into the test tube.

The bromothymol blue indicator changes color depending upon the pH or acid-base strength in a solution. When the acidic hydrogen ions formed at the positive terminal, the indicator was yellow. When the basic hydroxide ions formed at the negative terminal, the indicator was blue.

Both the sodium sulfate and the acid act as taxis for the electrons. Water by itself is a pretty good insulator, but if you put these things into it they will allow the electricity to do its job. The hydrogen gas is flammable and the oxygen gas helps flammable materials burn.

Questions to Ask

1. What was happening to the water to cause the bubbles to form at the ends of the wires?
2. Why did bubbles form at both wires and not just one?
3. Try the experiment without adding the sodium sulfate or acid and see what happens. What do these different compounds allow the electricity to do?
4. Turn the room lights out and see if you can tell what colors the two gases produce when they are ignited.
5. Can this experiment be repeated using a different kind of wire or does it have to be copper?

FINDING ELECTROLYTES

Activity

Different substances and solutions are tested for their abilities to conduct electricity.

Materials

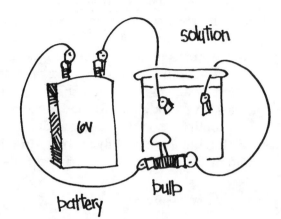

1 battery (with clip if you have one)
3 alligator clips
1 bulb with lamp
1 glass or plastic jar, 12 oz. is fine
    Samples of the following materials (not a finite list)

water	vinegar	baking soda
salt	lemon juice	sugar
orange juice	ammonia	oil

Construction and Use

1. Hook two of the alligator clips up to the battery clip, being careful to hook strictly to the terminal. Insert a lamp and clip, using the diagram as a guide. This should give you two free leads. Touch the leads together to make sure that the bulb and the battery are in working order before we continue.

2. Fill the jar with test solution number one and insert the two electrodes. If the light bulb lights up you have an electrolyte. If it doesn't, you don't. Continue to test the different solutions in the same manner.

What's Goin' On?

An electrolyte is, by definition, any substance that can become an ionic conductor of electricity when it is dissolved in a solvent, such as water. Once that substance is in the water, it facilitates the movement of the electrons as ions through the water from terminal to terminal so that there is a continuous current of electricity.

Questions to Ask

1. Make a list of the things that were good conductors of electricity and the things that were poor conductors and see if there are any patterns that develop.
2. Why does the electricity flow through some solutions and not others?
3. What happens if you mix an electrolyte with a non-electrolyte and run a current through it? Why do you think this happens?
4. Can the electricity move both directions in an electroyte? How did you prove this?
5. Do a little research and find out what electrolytes are used for and how they are used commercially.

COPPER ELECTROPLATING

Activity

A metal object is coated with copper using electricity.

Materials

1   empty milk carton
1   copper strip
1   shiny metal key
2   alligator clips
1   6 volt battery
     salt
     vinegar

Construction and Use

1.   Hook one alligator clip to each battery terminal and then clip the copper strip to the positive lead and the key to the negative lead.

2.   Fill the milk carton half full with vinegar. Now add salt to the vinegar a little at a time, stirring until the salt will no longer dissolve into the vinegar. This is a saturated solution.

3.   Place the key on one side of the milk carton and the copper strip on the other side and let it sit. Hydrogen bubbles will accumulate on the key and should be wiped off periodically to keep the reaction moving along at a nice clip.

What's Goin' On?

Electroplating was discovered by a scienctist named Michael Faraday. What happens is the copper is dissolved from the strip and is driven across the solution to the key, where it is deposited. At the same time, hydrogen is being released from the water as a gas.

Questions to Ask

1.   Where does the copper that is deposited on the key come from?

2.   What is the importance of putting the vinegar and salt in the water? What happens if you don't put them into the solution before you start?

3.   If you add another battery in series does the reaction proceed at an accelerated rate?

4.   Make a solution of copper sulfate by adding sulfate crystals to water until no more will dissolve. Instead of using a copper strip and a key, use two paperclips as the electrodes and put them in the solution. What happens?

5.   Where did the copper come from in the experiment just mentioned?

6.   Electroplating is used to coat many items of jewelry with a layer of gold. Have the kids collect samples and bring them in to display.

 Edison Etc.

LEMON BATTERY

Activity

A fresh lemon is crushed and rolled on the table top and two electrodes are inserted into the hide. The lemon is then attached to a galvanometer, which shows that an electric current is flowing.

Materials

1   large fresh lemon
2   alligator clips or pieces of copper wire, 20-22 gauge
1   roll of copper wire, 20-22 gauge
1   compass
1   piece of cardboard, 3 inches by 3 inches
1   roll of masking tape
1   paper clip or zinc strip, 3 inches by one half inch
1   piece of copper wire, 2 inches, or a copper strip the same size as the zinc

Construction and Use

1. Take one fresh lemon and squish it, roll it around on the table, and generally beat the lemon drippings out of the poor guy, just short of breaking the skin. You want to open up as many of the juice packets as possible.

2. Insert the copper and zinc electrodes into the lemon, making sure that they don't touch. An inch is a good distance to work with, although it doesn't hurt to experiment. If you don't have the copper and zinc strips then use the wire and the paper clip. If looks less official but it works just the same.

3. Attach wires to the electrodes (copper and zinc) and then construct a galvanometer.

4. A galvanometer is an instrument that measures a weak electric current. To make one of these puppies just lay the compass on the cardboard strip. If you put a small piece of tape on the back of the compass first, it will help. Then wrap a 6 foot piece of copper wire around and around the compass. Use the diagram for reference. Tape the wire together so it doesn't jump out all over the place and attach one end of the galvanometer to each of the test leads.

5. When you hook the wires to the test leads you will notice a deflection in the compass needle. This denotes a weak magnetic current.

What's Goin' On?

The copper electrons reacts with the acids in the lemon to form copper ions. These ions interact with the zinc electrode and steal electrons, forming zinc ions. This chemical reaction produces slightly over a volt of electricity. As the electrons move through the circuit, a weak magnetic field is produced, which causes the compass to move or deflect.

LEMON BATTERY

Questions to Ask

1. Why do you think we use two different kinds of metal?
2. Why do we use metal at all? Why not plastic or glass?
3. What happens to the compass if you take the wires and reverse them on the electrodes?
4. Do other kinds of citrus fruit produce the same effect? They should. Try orange, grapefruit and kiwi, for starters. Tangerines, tangelos, pineapples and kumquats (if you have small electrodes) also work well.
5. What about other kinds of fruit? Bananas, mangos, apples, or grapes (more small electrodes)?
6. What is it about the citrus fruit that makes it different from these other kinds of fruit?
7. Are there other metals that work just as well as copper and zinc? You will have to consult the periodic table of elements for this information or bug the high school chemistry teacher.
8. Can you put one electrode in one lemon and another in a second lemon and then connect the two lemons with a copper wire and get the same result?
9. Try the experiment with two electrodes of the same metal and see what happens. Have the kids find out what the difference is between an electron donor and electron acceptor.

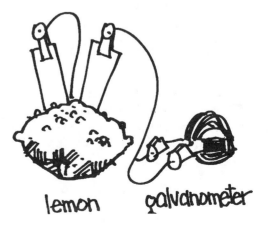

lemon   galvanometer

THE ELECTRIC POTATO

An electric current is run through a freshly cut, raw potato. The kids will observe a discoloration at one electrode and bubbling at the other.

Materials

1   fresh potato
1   knife
1   6 volt battery
2   feet of copper wire
1   phenolphthalein powder/ solution

Construction and Use

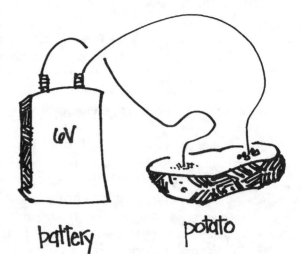

1. Cut the wire in half and hook one end of each wire to a terminal of the battery.
2.
    Add some phenolphthalein powder or a couple drops of solution to the surface of the potato.
3. Cut your potato in half and insert both wires into it about an inch apart. You will notice that the end that is connected to the negative lead will turn a greenish color and the end that is connected to the positive end will bubble or may have no reaction at all.

What's Goin' On?

That's a dang good question. You will notice that there is a greenish color forming at the positive electrode and a pink color forming at the negative electrode. The greenish color is due to the copper atoms ionizing from the wire to make cupric ions. The pink color at the negative electrode is due to phenolphthalein, an acid-base indicator, reacting with basic hydroxide ions. There are also bubbles of gas that form at the negative electrode. These are hydrogen bubbles from the hydrolysis or breaking apart of water molecules. This whole process requires about 1.2 volts of electricity to occur.

Questions to Ask

1. What the °&##ƒ! is going on here?
2. Why do you think the potato is starting to turn green and what are some of the reasons that it could turn green?
3. Are the bubbles made out of solid, liquid or gas?
4. Where do the bubbles come from?
5. What happens if you reverse the wires on the battery but do not take them out of the potato?
6. Are there other tubers and underground vegetables that produce the same effect? Try turnips, carrots, onions, different kinds of potatoes and, what the heck, garlic.

TOYS

A PRIMER

Time to play with all of these new ideas. This section takes the concepts and tools that we have learned and packages them into an entertaining form. Completed circuits now act as judges in contests of skill and nerves, signify correct answers to quizzes, and allow students to communicate in the tradition of the Old West, with Morse Code. Oh, and don't worry, you won't wind up looking like the kid below. It takes a lot of talent, more electricity than you have in a 6 volt lantern battery, and plenty of ink to look like that.

ELECTRIC MOTORS

Activity

An electric motor is made using electromagnets, a battery and a bit of patience.

Materials

2   ceramic magnets (either circular or square)
1   roll of copper wire, 20-22 gauge
4   thumbtacks
1   wire cutter
1   6 volt battery
2   alligator clips
1   wood block, 3" x 5" x 1/2 "
    masking tape

Construction and Use

1.   It is safe to say that in this particular instance a picture is going to be much more helpful that a whole pile full of directions. Nevertheless, cut six feet of copper wire and roll it into an oblong coil. Tape the sides of the coil with masking tape so that they will stay together. Make sure there are two 2 " strands.

2.   Cut two 6" pieces of wire and bend them into the cursive M shapes that you see in the diagram. These are the end supports for your motor. Thumbtack them down to the board.

3.   Cut two 4" lengths of wire and wrap them around the roll of wire that you wrapped earlier. When you have the whole thing wrapped, put it in the stand that you made in #2.

4.   Place the magnets under the wire loop and connect the two alligator clips to the battery and then one to each stand. Give the coil of wire a spin and you're off and running. If you have a hard time keeping it going, smoosh the stand down a little bit so that the coil is closer to the magnet.

What's Goin' On?

The coil of wire has an electric current running through it. When this happens a magnetic field is created around the wire coil. As the coil is given a spin, the magnet that was placed under it alternately attracts and repels the coil. The result is the spinning of the "motor".

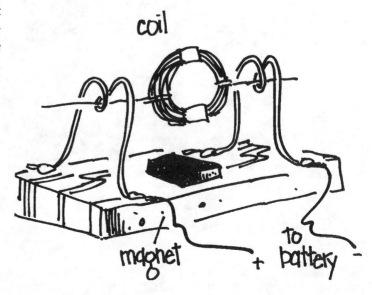

ELECTRIC MOTORS

Questions to Ask

1. Name the parts of this experiment that have electricity going through them. Name the parts of the experiment that an electrically induced magnetic field goes through. Note the differences. There should be none. This question is to get kids to think about induced magnetic fields.
2. Does the experiment work if you remove the magnets?
3. What direction does the motor spin if you reverse the magnet?
4. Remove the magnet at the bottom and hold two bar magnets on either side of the coil and tell what happens.
5. Reverse the alligator clips but keep everythng else the same and see what happens to the direction in which the motor spins.

NERVE TESTER

Activity

This is a fun device that tests the steadiness of a person's hand. If the loop touches the wire that is being navigated, a bulb will light up.

Materials

1   6 volt battery
3   alligator clips
1   bulb and socket
1   old wire coat hanger or 12 gauge copper wire, bare
2   thumbtacks or wood screws
1   piece of wood, 3" x 10" x 1/2 "

Construction and Use

1. Take a coat hanger wire and bend it into a wonderfully obnoxious shape. There is no set pattern for this but you can use the drawing for ideas. Thumbtack each end into the wooden base that you have.

2. Hook one alligator clip to each of the two battery terminals. Attach one lead to the thumbtack and the other lead to a 10- inch piece of copper wire with a loop on the end of it. At this point you have basically constructed the nerve tester. Check the diagram to see how close you are.

3. Start at one end and work your way to the other end. The objective is to go from one side to the other without touching the wire loop in your hand to the wire that is attached to the board.

What's Goin' On?

When the wire loop touches the large wire it completes the circuit and the light comes on.

Questions to Ask, Things to Try

1. What causes the light to go on when you touch the big wire with the loop?

2. Place a buzzer in the spot where the light is now and use the tester.

3. Construct two identical nerve testers and have races. One way to score the race is to have two stop watches and time the contestants. Each time the light comes on or the buzzer buzzes they are penalized one second.

4. Reverse the alligator clips; does it make a difference?

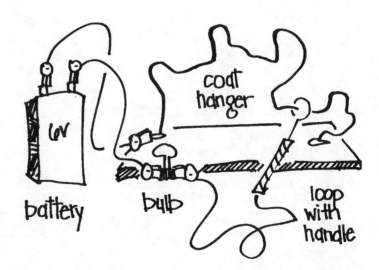

TELEGRAPH

Activity

The kids use their knowledge of electromagnets and circuits to make a telegraph that will send and receive messages tapped in code.

Materials

1   6 volt battery
1   paper clip
1   roll of copper wire, insulated, 20-22 gauge
6   thumbtacks
1   brad
1   pair of wire cutters
1   wood block 2" x 3" x 1/2"
1   wood block 3" x 10" x 1/2"
1   wood block 3" x 3" x 1/2"
1   strip of cardboard 1" x 3"
1   hammer
1   box of small finishing nails

Construction and Use

1.   Nail the 3" x 3" x 1/2" block onto the largest block so that it looks like the picture on this page. This is the base for the telegraph sounder.

2.   Make an electromaget using the nail and the wire. If you don't know how to do this please refer to the activity on page 45 of this book. Once you have finished the magnet, nail it into the center of the largest wooden block.

3.   Thumbtack the cardboard strip to the top of the sounder and insert another thumbtack upside down so that it is centered over the head of the electromagnet nail.

4.   Take a paperclip and bend it out into an S shape. See diagram and tack it down onto the third piece of wood using two thumbtacks. This is your switch.

5.   To hook the whole thing up connect one wire from the battery terminal to the thumbtack on the switch and another wire from the other terminal to the telegraph sounder. Finally, a third wire needs to be connected from the sounder to the switch.

6.   To operate your telegraph, simply push the paperclip down until it touches the thumbtack, completing the circuit.

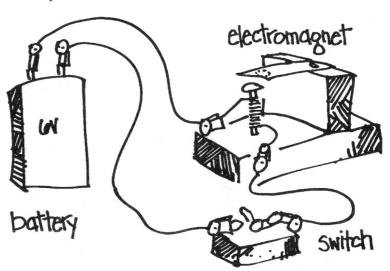

TELEGRAPH

What's Goin' On?

By pushing down on the switch you close the circuit. As the electricity flows through the circuit it energizes the electromagnet. Once the electromagnet becomes activated, it pulls on the thumbtack suspended in the cardboard, making a clicking sound. When the switch is released the electricity stops flowing, the electromagnet releases the thumbtack, and it is ready for the circuit to close again.

Questions to Ask, Things to Do

1. What causes the thumbtack to be attracted to the electromagnet?
2. Why is the elecromagnet important to this tool?
3. Learn Morse Code and send messages to one another.
4. Invent your own message code and send messages to other people.

Morse Code							
A	•—	K	—•—	U	••—	1	•————
B	—•••	L	•—••	V	•••—	2	••———
C	—•—•	M	——	W	•——	3	•••——
D	—••	N	—•	X	—••—	4	••••—
E	•	O	———	Y	—•——	5	•••••
F	••—•	P	•——•	Z	——••	6	—••••
G	——•	Q	——•—	,	——•——	7	——•••
H	••••	R	•—•	.	•—•—•—	8	———••
I	••	S	•••	?	••——••	9	————•
J	•———	T	—	'	•————•	0	—————

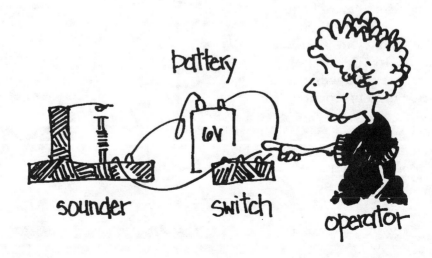

QUIZ BOARD

Activity

The kids will be able to make a self-testing quiz board that will allow them to write and match questions with answers.

Materials

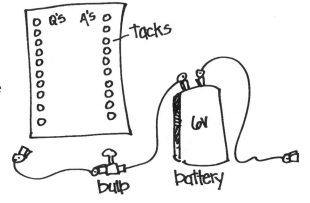

1   box of paper clips or thumbtacks
1   sheet of cardboard
1   roll of copper wire, insulated, 20-22 gauge
1   pair of wire cutters
1   battery with battery clip
1   bulb and socket

Construction and Use

1. Place 10 paperclips or thumbtacks along each side of a sheet of cardboard.
2. Attach three wires or alligator clips to the battery and bulb as pictured on the page.
3. The next task is to have the kids write ten questions with ten answers, type them up, cut them out, and put them on a page in a random order. Questions on the left and answers on the right.
4. Cut ten pieces of insulated wire, about 10 inches long, and strip the coating from the ends. Starting with question 1, connect the wire to the paper clip and then find the correct answer and connect the other end to that paperclip. This is done on the back of the cardboard, of course. Do this for all ten questions.
5. The way that you use the quiz board is to touch the one lead to the question that you want to answer. Read the possibilities and touch the other lead to what you think the answer is. If you are correct you will see the light go on.

What's Goin' On?

When the correct answer is matched to the appropriate question the circuit is completed and the light will go on.

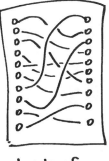

back of board

Van de Graff Generator

A Primer

The Van de Graff generator was invented to produce large static electric charges. The idea is really simple. A rubber belt spins in an acrylic cylinder. As it does this, it gathers electrons from the felt pulley at the bottom of the generator and the air. The electrons ride around on the belt until they go into the large metal ball on the top of the generator. As the belt goes over the top, the electrons are scooped off by a wire screen just above the belt and then the electrons are transferred to the large metal ball. The ball is where the charge accumulates until another conductor is brought close enough that the electrons can discharge onto it.

As you do the experiments you will notice white blue sparks jumping from the surface of the ball to objects that are brought close to it. According to the makers of the machine, you can calculate 25,000 volts for each inch the spark jumps, and on a dry day it is possible to reach voltages of over 300,000.

HAIRDO EXTRAORDINAIRE

Activity

Student of your choice is going to place their hand on the generator and collect enough electrons to make their hair stand on end.

Materials

1   Van de Graff generator
1   kid with shoulder length, fine hair, no mousse, gel or spray
1   insulating stand
1   rubber balloon (optional)

Construction and Use

1.   Have the volunteer stand on the insulating stand and place their hand on top of the generator which you have not turned on yet.
2.   Now you can turn on the generator.

What's Goin' On?

The generator is pumping out gobs of electrons, tons of the little buggars, and they are clammoring to get off the ball. Since your volunteer is touching the ball and the body is an excellent conductor of electricity, they race off the generator and onto her body.

As the electrons cover the body of your volunteer, they race from top to bottom looking for another place to go (electrons are transient like that) and find none. The insulating stand prevents the electrons from jumping down into the earth so they race back up to the head.   As the hair gets more and more electrons, it develops a negative charge. As more and more electrons migrate to the head of your volunteer, the greater the negative charge becomes. Each piece of hair now has a negative charge. Like charges repel so the hair follicles stand up on end to get away from the other hair follicles that also have a negative charge.

Questions to Ask

1.   Why does the hair stand on end?
2.   Where do the electrons come from?
3.   What happens if you don't stand on the insulating stand?
4.   Is the response any different if you just hold your hand over the ball instead of touching it?
5.   Test several people and decide which kind of hair works best.

EXPLODING PAPER

Activity

A pile of paper squares is placed on the generator before it is turned on. Once the generator is turned on the paper squares explode off the top of the ball and fly out into the room. Messy.

Materials

1   Van de Graff generator
1   pile of paper squares, quarter-inch square or so

Construction and Use

1.   Cut a whole pile of little chunks of paper just like the ones that you cut for the second activity in the book, Jumping Paper. They should be roughly a quarter inch square, not much bigger. Or, if you have those little circles from a paper punch, they work great and are just as hard to clean up.

2.   Place the pieces of paper on top of the Van de Graff generator. If the generator is on at this point it will be very difficult for you to do this. Turn the generator off and follow directions more carefully. The paper should just sit there with an occasional escapee down the side due to little to no friction.

3.   Turn the generator on and go get the broom and dust pan.

What's Goin' On?

When the paper is placed on top of the generator everything is in equilibrium. The paper is balanced and the generator is balanced. When you turn the generator on it messes the whole show up. The big metal ball gets a huge negative charge on it. These electrons, not content to stay where they are, jump onto the paper. Negative generator, negative pieces of paper. Like charges repel and you can take it from here.

Questions to Ask

1.   Why didn't the paper jump off when the generator wasn't running?

2.   Why did the paper not jump off the instant the generator was turned on? Why did it take a couple of seconds to get going ?

3.   What caused the paper to jump off, anyway?

4.   Does this kind of thing happen with all kinds of paper or just the kind that we used?

5.   Does anything else jump off the top of the generator or is it just paper? How about cloth, wood shavings, plastic straws cut into little bits or dead ants? Use dried ones; they are easier to clean up.

SCARED RABBIT

Acitivty

The kids will observe the effect of static electricity on a rabbit hide.

Materials

1   Van de Graff generator
1   rabbit hide without the rest of the rabbit in it

Construction and Use

1.   Lay the rabbit on top of the generator and have one kid come up and inspect the fur. Ask them to describe it.

2.   Once that is complete, turn the generator on and have them describe the rabbit fur once again. The fur should stick straight up into the air and the hide sometimes even flies off the sphere. Good fun.

What's Goin' On?

The hide accumulates tons of electrons in a short period of time. These electrons all have a negative charge. As they race out to the ends of each rabbit fur they recognize that the rabbit fur next to them has the same charge. Like charges repel and we have a rabbit fur of the excited state.

Questions to Ask

1.   Why does the fur stand on end when the generator is on, but does nothing when it is off?

2.   What happens when you move your hand over the surface of the rabbit fur but do not touch it? Why do you think this happens?

3.   Once the rabbit fur loads up on electrons where do they go?

4.   Flip the fur upside down and see what happens.

5.   Hold the fur over the generator instead of putting it directly on top and see how this influences the experiment.

LIGHTING THE BULB

Activity

A fluorescent bulb is brought near the generator and light is given off when static sparks hit the bulb. The experiment is repeated with an ordinary light bulb that does not glow at all.

Materials

1   Van de Graff generator
1   fluorescent bulb
1   standard electric bulb
1   dark room

Construction and Use

1.   Have a volunteer hold the fluorescent bulb near the generator and then the small electric bulb. Nothing should happen when either of these is brought near the generator. If by chance you do get one of them to light you are either doing something grossly incorrect or you have discovered a new scientific principle.

2.   Turn the light out in the room and fire up the generator.

3.   Have the kid hold the small electric light bulb near the generator. The spark should hit the bulb and then travel directly to the kid, without lighting the bulb too much. There may be a faint glow.

4.   Now have the kid hold the bottom (but not the end) of the long fluorescent tube. The tube can be burned out or still in good useable order, doesn't matter; the length is of no consequence either. Ask them to bring the tube close to the generator and hang on tight. I say hang on tight not because there is a shock that they can feel, but the light startles them and they drop the bulb.

What's Goin' On?

The inside of the glass bulb is coated with a white material called phosphor. Phosphor gives off light whenever it is struck by ultraviolet rays. The inside of the bulb is filled with a gas called mercury vapor, which gives off ultraviolet rays when it is excited with electricity. That pretty much sets the stage for the explanation.

LIGHTING THE BULB

When the bulb is brought close to the generator, a huge pile of electrons rip through the tube and go out the other side. As these electrons cruise through the tube they collide with the mercury vapor, which releases ultraviolet rays that strike the phosphor-emitting light. Ooooooh aaaaaaah. Or you could lie and say that it was a magic power that you have and the same power causes the hair to fall out of all noisy children. This is not conducive to the building of sound scientific minds, though.

The standard electric bulb is an evacuated glass bulb that is lit when the wire (also called the filament) has electricity passing through it. If you look carefully, the bulb will show off a little light, but nothing like the fluorescent bulb.

Questions to Ask, Things to Try

1. Why do you think the fluorescent bulb lit up and the regular bulb didn't?
2. Rest the bulb on the generator and see what happens.
3. Touch the very end of the bulb to the generator and see what happens to it.
4. How does the intensity of the light that is emitted from the bulb compare with the distance that the bulb is from the generator?
5. Stand on the insulating stand and do the experiment and then try it again on the floor.
6. When you hold the bulb close to the generator, you should feel a mild pull toward the generator when the spark strikes the bulb. What do you think causes the pull?

Human Circuit

Activity

The kids hold hands and form a living circuit. A person not in series with the generator acts as a ground and touches the kids on the nose, ear, and chin, and discharges the electricity that has accumulated in them.

Materials

1   Van de Graff generator
3   kids (more if you want)
1   darkened room for effect

Construction and Use

1.   Have kid number 1 put his or her hand on the generator and then start it up. This alleviates the need to shock the child at the outset.

2.   Once the generator is rolling along at a pretty good clip, ask the kid who is holding onto it to tilt their head back and look at the ceiling. If the room is dark this is even more dramatic. Touch the nose of the kid with your finger and a small blue spark will jump to your finger. The kid will feel a bit of a shock and everyone has a good laugh.

3.   You can touch them on the ear, cheek, neck, anywhere and draw a shock. Have the second kid hold hands with the first kid. There will be a little shock so have them grab hands quickly. The second kid can now be touched any of a number of places and draw a spark from them.

4.   You can add a third kid and as many as 30 kids, depending on the weather and, oddly enough, the kids. Occasionally you will get a kid who will not conduct a current. It is really odd. Also, the weather plays an important part in this and all static electricity experiments.

What's Goin' On?

The electricity is conducted through the kids just as if they were copper wires. There is more resistence in the body of a person than is in a wire, but the concept is the same. When a kid in the chain (or circuit) is touched by someone not in the circuit, it grounds it out temporarily. When you get too many people in the circuit, it won't work anymore because too much electricity is being lost as it travels through the circuit.

Human Circuit

Questions to Ask/Things to Do

1. Why was the first person who held onto the generator shocked?

2. Why could you touch the person anywhere and draw an electric shock?

3. Put a piece of paper between the nose of the kid on the generator and your finger. Does the paper insulate you from receiving a shock?

4. If the second person hooked into a generator lets go of the first is there a shock? Why or why not?

5. What happens if everyone keeps holding hands while the person touching the generator lifts their hand up and down and up and down? This is a great one if you want to hook up a bunch of your more pestiferous kids.

IONIC WIND

Activity

A lit candle is held near the generator. As it is brought closer, the flame bends toward it rather than going straight up.

Materials
1 Van de Graff generator
1 book of matches
1 candle
1 room without a draft (air, not military)

Construction and Use

1. Light a votive candle. These are those little, stubbie suckers the Catholics light when they are thinking of a friend. Hold the candle near the center of the generator. Ask the kids to observe the flame. If you are following directions you have not turned the generator on yet. If you are not following directions, why not? Turn the generator off and try again. The flame should go straight up.

2. Now fire up the old Van de Hoover and let it accumulate a charge. I would just turn it high enough to get the show rollin; if you crank it up you're gonna take a shock to the knuckles, spill hot wax on your hand, and get really mad at me and I don't want to hear about it. About half speed should by fine.

3. Once the generator is going, bring the candle close to the center of it again. You may want to wipe the wax off the generator when you are done.

What's Goin' On?

The generator has a considerable effect on the air particles surrounding it. They become charged, or ionized. When this happens, there is a movement set up that is visible with the flame of the candle, which is subject to the movement of the air particles in the room. Way cool, dudes.

Questions to Ask? Things to Do

1. Why is the flame going straight up the first time you hold it next to the generator and sideways the second time?

2. Does the experiment work the same with a match?

3. Try the experiment with fine threads and see if they also move in the same direction.

PUNK GENERATOR

Activity

A tissue paper attachment is constructed and placed on top of the generator. When it is turned on, it looks like a sea anenome or palm tree waving back and forth.

Materials

1   Van de Graff generator
1   roll of masking tape
1   sheet of tissue paper, at least 10" x 4"

Construction and Use

1.   Cut the sheet of tissue paper so that it is 10 inches long and 4 inches wide.
2.   Cut half inch wide strips almost the length of the paper. When you are done you should have eight strips of paper roughly 9 1/2 inches long, attached at the base.
3.   Fold the base of the tissue paper in half, lengthwise, three times and tape the end closed. When you are done you should have what resembles an anemic pom pom.
4.   Tape the bottom, or handle, of the pom pom to the top of the generator and turn the generator on.

What's Goin' On?

As the static charge builds up the electrons accumulate on the pieces of tissue paper. Since each strip is absorbing a huge negative charge and like charges repel, the tissue strips can't stand each other and "fly" up into the air to get as far from each other as possible. It would be interesting to be able to see the magnetic lines of force in one of these experiments; probably looks worse than the LA freeway system.

Questions to Ask/ Things to Do

1.   Why are the strips flying up into the air?
2.   Where is the static charge coming from to create this phenomenon?
3.   What happens if you use thinner strips? Fatter?
4.   Does the experiment work as well if you tape the palm to the side of the generator? What about the underside?
5.   Will this experiment work if you hold the palm tree on top of the generator instead of taping it?
6.   Does electrical tape work better than masking tape? How does scotch tape rate, or does it? Duct tape? Duck tape? General all purpose aviary tape? Just kidding on the last two.
7.   Hold the palm tree by the handle upside down over the generator. What happens? Now stand on an insulating stand. Any difference?

THE SPARK

Activity

The kids will observe and, if they choose, experience a several thousand volt charge striking their bodies. No harm, just a little jolt.

Materials

1   Van de Graff generator
1   brave kid
1   light switch

Construction and Use

1.   Plug the machine in and let it warm up for a minute or two. It will need some time to generate a charge. For best effect darken the room.

2.   Once the machine has started to crackle and fizz (an electric charge has begun to accumulate), have the kid make a fist and approach the generator like Frankenstein. This is more for effect than relating to anything that is at all scientific. When the kid gets close enough, depending on the weather, a bright blue spark will jump from the generator to the kid's fist. This will undoubtedly cause the kid to whirl and jump back, but there is no danger to the kid at all. Just a nice healthy jolt to the hand, no burns or scars.

What's Goin' On?

As the electrons accumulate on the generator they start to get crowded. I tell the kids that it is just like cramming a bunch of them into their bathroom at home. They wouldn't like it and they would be looking for a way out. The electrons are the same way. The more crowded it gets the more likely they are to jump off. That's why you have to let the generator warm up for a bit first.

As the kid approaches the generator the electrons recognize a conductor when they see one, and when it is within the bounds of science they jump ship and discharge onto the kid. The charge is quickly dispersed through the entire body and down into the floor.

Questions to Ask/ Things to Try

1.   Why didn't the spark jump to the kid when he was further away?

2.   Why does the machine pause in between sparks? Another way to pose that question: Why isn't there a continuous stream of electricity, rather than a spark?

3.   What happens if the kid puts his hand on the generator and leaves it there and another kid tries to draw a spark from the generator?

4.   What is happening to all of the electrons in question 3?

5.   Approach the generator with an open palm. Then try an elbow; noses not recommended.

6.   Hold your finger two inches, one inch, and a half an inch away from the generator and compare the size, intensity and frequency of the sparks.

ABOUT THOMAS ALVA EDISON

A brief chronology of the life of Mr. Edison is given for bulletin board ideas, essay topics and general informational puposes. It's the way he would have wanted it.

1847   He was born in Milan, Ohio on February 11 to Samuel and Nancy Elliot Edison.

1862   Printed and published a newspaper, The Daily Herald; the first one to ever be published on a train.

1863   Began a five year period as a telegraph operator. Liked to tinker and improve the idea.

1870   Received his first money for an invention, $40,000 for his stock ticker paid by the Gold and Stock Telegraph Company. He opened a manufacturing shop in Newark and made the instruments.

1872   Worked on the following inventions: motograph, automatic telegraph system, duplex, quadruplex, and multiplex telegraph systems. He also worked on parafin paper and the carbon rheostat.

1875   Invented the automatic copying machine, which he sold to A.B. Dick of Chicago. We call the machine a mimeograph.
1876   Established the first industrial park devoted to research.

1877   Applied for a patent on the carbon telephone transmitter, which made the telephone commercially practicable. It included the microphone, which is used in radio broadcasting.

1877   Invented the tin foil phonograph. It was the first time a machine has recorded and played sound.

1878   First meeting of Edison Electric Lighting Company. The following year invented the incandescent bulb. It operated for more than 40 hours.

1879   Invented radical improvements in the construction of dynamos, sockets, switches and fuses for the regulation, distribution and measurement of electric current.

1880   This year ushered in an era of invention and patent applications for the scientist. Over the course of his lifetime he applied for and received 1093 patents. 365 of these were for electric lighting and power distribution.

1883   Filed for a patent on an electrical indicator using the Edison Effect. This was the first patent in the science now known as electronics.

1889   Showed an experimental motion picture that was synchronized with a phonograph player.

1891-1931   Invented the grandfather of the modern motion picture camera, ore extraction processes, coal tar experiments that led to development of explosives, and refined his inventions of movie cameras and telegraph and telephone systems. Your basic busy inventor.

1931   Died in West Orange, New Jersey at the age of 84.

A Brief History of Electrical Discoveries

2637 B.C.   According to Chinese legend, a magnetic chariot was used by the founder of the empire, Hoang-ti.

1650   First static machine was built by the German physicist, Otto van Guericke. It produced static electricity by rubbing a pad against a large rotating sulphur ball.

1729   Theory of conductors and nonconductors , later leading to the discovery of electrical insulation, was conceived by Stephen Gray, an English experimenter.

1745   Leyden jar principle was discovered by Pieter van Musschenbrock of Holland, showing how charges of static electricity can be built up and stored.

1747   Lightning rod was invented by Benjamin Franklin, along with the single fluid theory of electricity, and "plus" and "minus" designations.

1771   Theory of "animal electricity" originated when Luigi Galvani used two dissimilar metals to touch a frog's legs and made them contract.

1800   Generation of electricity was first made practical by Allesandro Volta, who stacked silver and zinc plates, separated by cloth or paper, and saturated them with a salt solution. The "voltaic pile" bears his name.

1821   Michael Faraday showed that a wire carrying a current can revolve around a magnet, and can cause the magnet to revolve around it.

1823   An electric current was produced when Thomas Johann Seebeck joined two dissimilar metals and heated their junction point.

1827   George Simon Ohm showed that the resistance of a conductor is represented by the electromotive force divided by the rate of current flow through the conductor. Ohm's law showed the relationship between current, voltage, and resistance in an electric circuit.

1840   Telegraph invented by Samuel F. B. Morse.

1865   The transmission of electric and magnetic fields through a medium was explained by James Clerk Maxwell.

1875   Electric telephone was developed by Alexander Graham Bell.

1887   Electric energy given off by certain metals that had been struck by light was discovered by Heinrich Rudolph Hertz. The next year he discovered that electromagnetic waves can transmit electricity.

1888   Principle of the rotating magnetic field, grandfather of the induction motor, was discovered by Nicola Tesla.

BRIGHT IDEAS

BRIGHT IDEAS